The Ballroom Murder

Leigh Straw is an academic, historian and writer. She is the author of true crime biographies of Australian crime figures Kate Leigh and Dulcie Markham, and Australia's first female detective, Lillian Armfield, as well as *The Petticoat Parade: Madam Monnier* and the *Roe Street Brothels*. Leigh was joint winner of the 2018 Margaret Medcalf Award for her book *After the War: The Mental and Physical Scars of World War I*. Leigh Straw is Deputy Head of the School of Arts and Sciences and Associate Professor in History at The University of Notre Dame Australia.

The Ballroom Murder

The dancefloor shooting that shocked Australia

LEIGH STRAW

FREMANTLE PRESS

For Tony
You have given me a life lived with such great love and respect.
Thank you.

Also Caroline Ingram and Michael Adams
Thank you for your generous support with this project.
I am so very grateful.

Contents

Prologue: 'Flash of fire'   7

1. Fremantle Flapper   12
2. 'I see blood between you!'   20
3. '… to keep her own counsel'   28
4. 'The Remarkable Eyes of Audrey Campbell Jacob'   38
5. 'She appeared to be in a dazed condition'   47
6. '… to blacken the character of the deceased'   65
7. 'It is a deliberate case of wilful murder': The trial begins   75
8. '… things are not always what they may seem': The trial continues   85
9. 'In The Shadow of the Gallows': The verdict   99
10. 'I told him everything'   114
11. '… probable heart attack'   127

Appendix A: 'My Six Weeks in the Shadow of the Gallows!'   136

Acknowledgements   145

Notes   149

References   173

Prologue: 'Flash of fire'

They came from across the city, descending onto the grounds of Government House for the annual St John of God Hospital Ball on 26 August 1925. Some guests were in fancy dress, others in more formal attire. The day had hinted at the coming of spring with an eighteen-degree high but a coolness had descended on the evening. There was plenty of merriment as Sergeant William Brodie watched guests turning up from his vantage point at the bottom of the entrance to Government House. Brodie wasn't expecting anything out of the ordinary. Perth was more like a large country town, and the Government House job seemed pretty straightforward for a seasoned police officer like Brodie. There would probably be some drunken antics and maybe he would need to provide a gentle nudge later in the evening to guests who wanted an all-nighter. He had already alerted the younger officers to be on watch for this. All the same, he was not taking the evening's job lightly. Government House was the official residence of Western Australia's governor and there were a number of officers from the surrounding police stations working the late shift to bolster police numbers at the ball. Sergeant Brodie had positioned police officers at entry and exit points around the building and inside near the ballroom to emphasise the police presence. Officers included Constable John Wood, who was outside the ballroom with a good view of exit points. Constable Alfred George Timms, from Highgate

Hill Police Station, was keeping an eye out at the foot of the staircase at the back balcony.

As a city emerged around it, Government House still recalled its colonial past. It was a two-storey building that had been built in the middle of the nineteenth century in the Jacobean revival style. It had been renovated in the 1890s to include a ballroom and, since then, the mansion featured in major social events. The St John of God Ball was a favourite on the local calendar.

Guests arrived from the St Georges Terrace main entrance and followed the path bordered by expansive gardens which, to the right, led over to Stirling Gardens at the front of the Supreme Court building. Government House, with its red-orange brick, paler trim and distinctive turrets, was majestic, set against a developing modern city.

At half past eight, while guests came and went from the building, music floating out from open doors, Sergeant Brodie watched two young women arrive. Dressed in pantomime outfits, laughing and pulling each other along, they were obviously looking forward to an evening of fun. Brodie switched his attention back to canvassing the building once more.

In the coming hours and days ahead, Sergeant Brodie would wonder if there was anything he had missed about these two young women, and if there was anything he could have done to prevent the tragedy that would unfold in the early hours of the morning.

Twenty-year-old Audrey Jacob was dressed as the operatic male character Pierrot, matched to her friend Annie Humphreys' Pierrette outfit. In pantomime, theatre, opera and ballet, Pierrot is the naïve, unhappy clown—pining for the love of Clementine—but these two young women were merry and excited. They hurried inside the grand old building, passing by other guests walking down the hallway towards the ballroom. This was an expansive space, with an impressive arched ceiling and colonnaded balconies on two levels. The orchestra was already playing up one end, and Audrey and Annie began twirling each other in circles, caught up in their own world.

Audrey Jacob enjoyed the first hour of the ball, dancing and chatting with her friend, but her mood changed when she noticed a young man dancing nearby, and grabbed Annie's arm.

PROLOGUE: 'FLASH OF FIRE'

'Do you see him?' Audrey asked, pointing over and across the dancefloor.

It was Audrey's former fiancé, Cyril Gidley. He looked carefree and cheery, dancing and relishing the company of a number of young women.

'Just ignore him, Audrey,' Annie told her friend, but Audrey had lost interest in dancing. Annie convinced her to get some supper and it was there that they met another male guest and chatted over some food. Audrey seemed happy once again as the songs continued and Annie headed back to the dancefloor with their supper guest. The thirteenth song of the evening began: Gladys Moncrieff's popular hit from the year before, 'Follow Yvette'. Moncrieff was heralded as 'Australia's Queen of Song' and the mood on the dancefloor echoed this. But as Annie danced with her partner, Audrey left the dance area, solemn and withdrawn.

When the song ended, Annie went to find her friend. She hoped to see her in the hallway but grew increasingly worried when she didn't find her there. Nor was she in the cloakroom. Annie checked all the main areas but there was no sign of Audrey. Frantic now, she hurried back to the dancefloor but was pulled into a dance with another man. Circling around the ballroom, she looked for Audrey, hoping she was dancing with someone else.

Minutes later, Annie saw Audrey. She had discarded her fancy dress and was now wearing a stunning blue evening dress. Before they could talk, another man came along and whisked Annie away to dance. Distracted now by concerns for her friend and the time—it was one in the morning—Annie was anxious to leave. She lived a good thirty minutes away in Fremantle, unlike Audrey who had an apartment in the city. Annie caught sight of her friend again, this time up on one of the balconies. She was looking down over the ballroom. Looking for Cyril, thought Annie. She rushed up the staircase to Audrey.

'I need to leave and get my things from your room,' Annie told Audrey, hoping her friend might also want to leave the ball.

Audrey did not take her eyes off the dancefloor but told her friend where she would find the key to her room, back at Surrey Chambers. She then said she was going to talk to Cyril. Annie wondered if that was such a good idea but she doubted she could convince Audrey otherwise.

On her way out, Annie passed by the lounge and it was there that she saw Cyril with a female companion.

'Miss Jacob would like to speak to you,' she told him, pointing up to the balcony where Audrey was standing.

Cyril looked up, as did his dance partner.

'I'll go and see her soon,' he said.

From Government House, Annie walked the short distance to Surrey Chambers where Audrey had recently moved. This was a large building on the corner of St Georges Terrace and Howard Street, three blocks from Government House, and some of its rooms were let out to renters. Once in Audrey's room, Annie changed out of her costume for the ride home on public transport. She was optimistic she could still make the last charabanc to Fremantle.

Back at Government House, Audrey was waiting for Cyril to come and see her but he had decided instead to head back out onto the dancefloor with his partner. Maude Mitchell was a beautiful young woman who appeared to be enjoying Cyril's company very much indeed. As they laughed and danced their way through another song, Audrey descended the stairs from the balcony and walked across the ballroom floor towards Cyril.

No one saw the revolver she was holding as she wound through the throng. She stopped six feet away from him. The gun was now pointed at Cyril.

Then someone heard a 'flash of fire'. Guests close by screamed. The dancing stopped. So did the orchestra.

One man rushed to help. Perth doctor Sydney O'Neill knew the next few seconds were vital. He looked for others to help and soon there was a small crowd around Cyril.

Newspaper editor Victor Courtney was nearby too. He and his business partner, John Joseph Simons, had turned the *Mirror* into a popular local newspaper which delighted in titillating its readers with sensational headlines about scandals, particularly divorce cases. Courtney would find himself playing an instrumental part in the drama that was about to grip his city.

PROLOGUE: 'FLASH OF FIRE'

Hearing the crack, and the cries of the guests, Sergeant Brodie and other officers ran across the dancefloor from all directions. Their first actions were to secure the scene and check on the man lying on the floor. Dr O'Neill motioned for them to take the victim to the cloakroom. There, in the genteel surrounds of Government House, just minutes later, Cyril Gidley died.

1. Fremantle flapper

Audrey Jacob was driven from Government House to the police lock-up a few blocks away. Shortly after, a lawyer was engaged to represent her, and the police began their investigation into the murder of Cyril Gidley. Alone in her cell, Audrey waited to see what daylight would bring. Across the city, and down by the port, Audrey's family slept through the rest of the night not knowing that their lives would never be the same again.

The Jacob family lived at 592 High Street, Fremantle but they had moved around a fair bit since Edward and Jessie were married in Perth in 1902. They were both from Victoria—Edward was born in Collingwood in 1871 and Jessie was born in Hotham in 1878—but had met in Western Australia. Their first child, Rupert, was born in Victoria Park in 1903 before Audrey came along two years later on 9 February 1905. Her middle name, Campbell, was her grandmother's maiden name. Ann (née Campbell) and her husband, Colin Junner, had emigrated from Cromarty in the Scottish Highlands to Victoria in 1871 with Jessie's three elder siblings. Audrey would identify most with this Scottish heritage.

Edward and Jessie moved their young family to Collie in the Wellington District before another son, Clifton, was born in 1907. Three more children were born in this district—Keith (1909), Enid (1910) and Verna (1912)—before the Jacob family moved again, this

1. FREMANTLE FLAPPER

time to Dundas, a town near Norseman in the Goldfields–Esperance region. The last two Jacob children were born there, Vivienne in 1916 and Dudley in 1919. Within three years, they were back in the city, at South Fremantle and then at the High Street house. The family moved with Edward's work as a clerk of courts. The regional appointments gave him more experience for an ongoing city position.

In the early 1920s, Fremantle became their long-term home. It was a thriving port town known for its shipping, transport, wharfies and unions—a rough-diamond kind of a place. If you were going to have a scrape somewhere, it was probably going to be down in Fremantle. The locals stuck fast to one another and viewed visitors with some suspicion, especially if they came from Perth. Western Australia's two main centres had developed distinct characters over the decades. Perth was a 'shabby-genteel' place, whereas Fremantle was working-class and proud of this distinction. It didn't stop the press in Perth calling out Fremantle as a port of 'Beastly Backyards and Stinking Slums' and the kind of place where you could find a 'brothel between two churches'. And, as it turned out, you could; that was all part of its rugged charm.

Fremantle was a poorer part of the metropolitan area, with a greater concentration of small cottages and boarding houses in the inner streets. The wealthier favoured the riverside streets of North Fremantle and parts of East Fremantle along the Inner Harbour. South Fremantle came to be known as home to 'the racehorse and the battler', with limestone and wooden cottages also having stables out the back.

It could also be a rough, criminal place. Thieving gangs centred their attentions on the shipping sheds and yards, and the wharves provided dishonest lumpers with opportunities to steal items from cargo arriving regularly in the port. Police and Customs raids on houses in North Fremantle late in December 1902 failed to turn up six cases of tobacco stolen from the 'B' sheds at Victoria Quay.

But the harbour was not the only dodgy part of town. People were susceptible to attacks in alleys and laneways. In April 1924, the head of the Fremantle Criminal Investigation Branch expressed his concern in court that the absence of lights in the laneways behind businesses was 'an inducement to boys to embark upon careers of crime'. Speaking at the trial of three boys charged with stealing from Fremantle shops, he declared unlit lanes provided a cover of darkness for raids of shops, during what the paper termed a recent 'epidemic of thieving' in the port town.

Pakenham, Leake, Bannister and Market streets all featured regularly in criminal cases being reported in the newspapers. In an effort to deal with the problem of prostitution and houses of 'disreputable character', police raided a number of houses over the course of a weekend in May 1903. Houses in Norfolk, Arundel, Pakenham and Bannister streets were targeted and the police were commended in court soon after for trying to 'rid the town of its undesirable characters'.

But as rough and ready as it was, Fremantle was also a cosmopolitan place, flourishing from the gold rushes of the 1890s and the opening of the port soon after. An influx of immigrants and seamen from around the world clambered ashore in Fremantle. They came from China, Japan, Sweden, Germany, Britain and America, and regularly disembarked at Fremantle, enjoying the town's entertainments or taking the first steps towards a new life. Italians took to fishing in Fremantle and set up market gardens while other European food producers, many of them from Greece, established businesses along Market Street and South Terrace. Local workers and new arrivals with a thirst for beer also brought about the building of new pubs as a means to keep up with a rising clientele. By the 1920s, the P&O, National and Fremantle hotels were also bringing more young people into the port town.

The port captured the creative interest of a young Audrey Jacob. The views along the wharf and over the water were ideal for watercolours or acrylics, though both could be expensive and beyond what her parents could buy her. From her house on High Street she could catch a tram into Fremantle and wander along Phillimore Street and down to the port. The comings and goings of the place were fascinating: people arriving, others leaving, and always something happening.

1. FREMANTLE FLAPPER

Perhaps it was ingrained in her, this fascination with people moving about, travelling, arriving somewhere new. She had already moved several times in her young life and her grandparents were immigrants.

Audrey also experimented with self-portraits and, apparently, they were very good, lauded by those who saw her as gifted. This artistic ability may have come from her grandfather. Colin Junner was a painter before he emigrated to Australia, albeit a painter of buildings, houses, fences and properties—nonetheless, it took a creative eye to consider colours, texture and broader property appeal.

Edward Jacob was not supportive of his daughter's ambitions. He objected to Audrey wanting to become a professional artist. It was hardly going to pay the bills and, as one of the older children, it was on Audrey to help out at home with the cost of living. But it was the jaunts into town with friends which took Audrey into Fremantle's social life and worried her family more.

It was a fine time to be a young woman. This was the Roaring Twenties, which saw the ascent of the modern young woman, or 'flapper', as she came to be known. The flapper had been around since the late-nineteenth century but it was the post–World War One world which made this version of the modern woman famous. The tragedy and loss of war on a world scale left people looking to a new decade where they could try to overcome the burdens of that recent past. Young people in particular were hopeful for a better future free of war. Flappers wanted to break from the constraints of the past and push the boundaries of social expectations of femininity. They had already begun this process during the war, with more women entering into work in the vacuum created by men enlisting.

Flappers were not passive women, defining themselves by sexual purity and high morals. They were 'trouble' and enjoyed attention, living beyond convention. They usually started out at sixteen or seventeen years of age and were determined to stand out in society, especially in public. They smoked, danced late into the evening in clubs and at house parties, and were the cause of great concern in conservative circles. They defied conventions to embrace independent lifestyles.

Flappers experimented with colours and designs in their clothing, basking in youthful androgyny. The boyish shaping of dresses, with dropped waists to create straight contours, flattened the chest and hid hips. Dances of the time, many a variation on the Charleston, were best demonstrated in short, light dresses with no sleeves so that young women could move their arms more freely. The idea, even in the way they dressed and danced, was to proclaim that women could have their own identities.

Flappers found one of their greatest champions in the works of American writer F. Scott Fitzgerald. Fitzgerald's early works—*The Beautiful and Damned*, *This Side of Paradise* and *Flappers and Philosophers*—transformed the flapper into a literary symbol for the lost generation of the 1920s. She was powerful, complex and contradictory. Fitzgerald modelled the flapper on his young, exuberant and unconventional wife, Zelda, and gave young women an icon for the era they could relate to. And his works were being read and talked about in Perth and Fremantle, on the other side of the world.

Not everyone was keen to see this new modern woman out in public. The *Fremantle Advertiser* raised questions in January 1924 about 'unprotected' young girls being 'allowed to frequent the streets late at night' and asked for a curfew. Of particular concern were the sailors meeting the interests of the young women:

> In a port of this size, the danger is most acute. Sailors of a certain class, particularly those of different nationalities, are apt to judge by appearances. Girls parading the streets without proper protection are immediately classed by them as belonging to the lowest strata of society, and treated accordingly. The girls in the beginning, do not realise this aspect. They are eager for flattering attention, and with too much liberty, seek it in dangerous places. If the parents will not realise the seriousness of the position, the matter will soon be taken out of their hands.
>
> […] Somebody has suggested a "Curfew Bell" and an attendant patrol. It would seem to be in imminent need. In about a month, there will be an influx of British sailors to Fremantle, and while everybody will delight

in welcoming them, the lure of uniforms has always a most seductive effect upon many of our girls. The need for supervision will be doubled, and while we desire our hospitality to be of the highest grade, it must be our aim to see that it is in no way violated.

It was a common sight for young Fremantle women to be seen down at the port mingling with men from the ships, and the local press were particularly harsh about their antics:

When the Belgian barque which is now in the harbor leaves port, there will be much heartrending amongst the local flappers. Put a naval uniform on a good-looking monkey, and one would have the same results.

Audrey Jacob was a Fremantle flapper who enjoyed spending her spare time down at the port trying to attract the interests of the men working on the ships. She wasn't alone. Her friends were there too, vying for attention and entranced by the uniforms and worldly experience. Audrey wore her hair short, her lips red with lipstick and fashioned herself in the flapper fashions of the day, in stark contrast to the more conservative Edwardian look of her mother's youth. But Audrey was classically beautiful too and this was obvious even when dressed in the flapper fashions.

Audrey was young and wanted more independence. The men on the ships coming and going from Fremantle port seemed to promise adventure. Onboard for visits to the men, she could be appreciated for her beauty and artistic talents. There was always the hope of a private date with a captain who might whisk her off to some faraway, exotic place.

✦ ✦ ✦

Cyril Gidley was twenty-three when he arrived in Western Australia in 1923. He was a charismatic, good-looking young Englishman who had left Grimsby to work as a ship's engineer. His father, Joseph, worked as a fish merchant's clerk while Cyril and his brother and sister grew up, but was later said to have been a ship owner. Joseph and Florence had been keen for their son Cyril to pick up regular work. They hoped working as an engineer on ships would keep him busy and out of trouble. He was young, single and had a keen sense of adventure at a time when adventuring seemed possible again. It was the 1920s, after all.

Cyril's uncle Herbert lived in Newcastle, New South Wales but Cyril decided to head to Western Australia. He arrived in Bunbury, in the state's south, in April 1923, and worked on the steamer *Newquay* before he took ill shortly after. He relocated to Fremantle, much to the dismay of a young woman, with whom he had taken up. In Fremantle, he picked up work as an engineer on the motor ship *Kangaroo*, which travelled to Singapore every six weeks. Cyril enjoyed the company of a small group of close friends while he was in Fremantle, some with connections back in England, and others who worked with him on the ship.

There were rumours that Cyril had been kicked out of home in England, told by his parents that he could not return for five years until he had a steady job and turned his life around. The press would also circulate stories that Cyril had apparently brought some disgrace to his wealthy family, especially his father as a retired ship owner.

Cyril had a bit of form for causing a stir. Around April 1924, he had an argument on ship with another crew member. As the pair scuffled and fought, Cyril was hit in the stomach with a sledgehammer. He was taken to Bunbury Hospital where he was stitched up and told to take time off work. This was when he started seeing a young woman in town but their engagement was soon over. By the later winter months of 1924, Cyril was settling into life in Fremantle. His friend, a customs officer by the name of William Vincent Murphy, offered him a room in his house just outside Fremantle. The pair struck up a friendship and William's wife, Violet, also came to know Cyril well.

Free from his parents' supervision in England, and travelling the world, Cyril Gidley enjoyed his freedom. He was stylish, often seen with a cigarette held in a smiling mouth poised to impress the young ladies in the port city. His features were soft and yet his eyes were

1. FREMANTLE FLAPPER

intense. He stood out in the crowd, and it was in August of 1924 that he caught the eye of Audrey Jacob.

Over the course of that winter, Audrey and Cyril became friends and then started dating. They met on occasion at Cyril's friends' house where he stayed while on leave from the ship. Violet and William Murphy lived in Palmyra, not far from Audrey's home, but with enough distance that the young lovers would not be caught out. Audrey's parents were not keen on her meeting men from the ships down at the port. She also knew that someone who regularly spent weeks away would not necessarily meet her parents' approval. Especially her father.

As they wandered down by the port and around the streets, Cyril talked to Audrey about his family back in England and how he was looking to make a new start. Audrey mentioned her love of art and how she wanted to be a professional painter. To anyone who saw them in the early days of their relationship, it looked as if Audrey and Cyril were young and in love.

But before too long, cracks would start to show.

2. 'I see blood between you!'

> There is one story however, which, while not necessarily affecting the tragedy in any way, will be of interest to those who believe in Fate, and the possibility of delving into the future.
> *Mirror,* 12 September 1925.

Audrey Jacob may have thought herself in love with Cyril Gidley, but perhaps she didn't feel entirely secure about their relationship. A story would later circulate that Audrey and Cyril had gone to see a fortune-teller together. Perhaps Audrey had questions she wanted answered. What did Cyril get up to when he was away in Singapore for weeks at a time? Who was the woman in Bunbury he had been involved with?

In the first decades of the twentieth century, the need for certainty about love led many young women across Australia to consult clairvoyants and fortune-tellers, to know if a relationship was right for them, or whether their suspicions about infidelity were true. But like so many other young women at the time, it is possible that Audrey had little idea of the stigma associated with the work and the efforts of the police to crack down on the business. She wasn't alone. Clairvoyants and fortune-tellers were popular in Australia by the first decades of the twentieth century. Their clients, more often than not, were young women hoping for love. The need for certainty about love led many young women across Australia to consult people claiming to be able to predict the future.

Fortune-tellers and clairvoyants mainly worked from the back rooms of their houses but were also available for house visits. Some worked door to door, and in market stalls and small shops. Their work included card and palm readings, crystal-gazing, reading tea leaves and the less common reading of heads, faces, fingernails and personal objects. Fortune-tellers were less interested in communication with the spirit world. Fortune-tellers were usually women, though men also engaged in the work. It was more usual for women to see female clients and male fortune-tellers to see men.

These days we tend to view fortune-telling and clairvoyance as relatively harmless services where clients engage with future predictions and spiritualism, anywhere from individual consultations to psychic events and hen's parties. But back in the early twentieth century, fortune-telling was seen as a fraudulent business and it was criminalised in the belief that it was intended to rip people off. Complaints were made to police when fraud was suspected and the police acted under legislation to apprehend suspected fortune-tellers.

Fortune-tellers could be charged with obtaining money through false pretences under section 66 (later repealed) of the Western Australian *Police Act 1892*. They were also charged as 'rogues and vagabonds' in relation to making false statements or representations. Police could seek a conviction of up to six months in prison for '[e]very person pretending to tell fortunes, or using any subtle craft, means, or device, to deceive and impose upon any person'.

'Pretence' was a major issue in cases against fraudulent fortune-tellers. Often referred to as 'charlatans' in the newspapers, fortune-tellers were investigated when they appeared to be acting professionally but were really conning people out of their money with false predictions. There were various police raids launched across the city on a regular basis from the late nineteenth century and particularly during World War One when anxious girlfriends, wives and families wanted to know about loved ones fighting overseas.

In July 1917, four women and one man appeared in Perth Police Court charged with having pretended to tell fortunes. Operating individually out of their houses on Wellington, Pier and Francis streets in the city centre, their business activities came under the watchful eyes of detectives Condon and Doyle. They were particularly interested in Catherine Hill's house, as she already had form for fortune-telling.

Two female clients were approached by the detectives and taken to the police station to provide statements about Catherine Hill's business on Wellington Street. Their evidence confirmed fortune-telling work so Condon and Doyle returned to the house, only to find a note on the front door saying Mrs Hill was in Fremantle and would see 'no strangers, only special friends' on her return. The problem was, Mrs Hill had been spotted five minutes later. She denied that she knew anything about fortune-telling. The evidence in court pointed to Mrs Hill having charged a half-crown to tell the fortunes of the two women by card and hand. She spread the cards out on the table, asked one to wish, and said she would get her wish. Then came the predictions:

> She told me I would be going on a water journey ... She said I would hear of the death of a fair relation of my mother's, and that I would travel more than "I had expected to." ... She asked me to wish again. She said I would hear of a little boy's death that would upset me very much, and that I would have a removal that I would not regret; she told me I would get a letter and a telegram, which were not expected, and would hear of a boy's death at the war.

Inspector Walsh, who was conducting the prosecution, asked the witness if she actually wished for anything. She laughed, replying, 'Yes, and I have not had the things yet.' She also confirmed that none of what had been predicted had come true. Her friend, who had also seen the fortune-teller, gave evidence that Mrs Hill told her she would get a present from a 'fair boy' she loved at the front. Catherine Hill was convicted and fined.

2. 'I SEE BLOOD BETWEEN YOU!'

The police generally accepted fortune-telling work if it was kept private and didn't interfere with the local community, but fortune-tellers were often stereotyped as associating with thieves and criminal gangs. Fraudulent fortune-tellers coaxed information out of clients that could be sold on to thieves who would use it to break into homes or workplaces. Clients might, for example, give information about work hours and forthcoming holidays that would leave their business or home vacant.

Women were viewed as easy prey for fortune-tellers. Newspaper reporters claimed that because women were more likely to engage in gossip—a favourite pastime of theirs, apparently—this made them an easy target for wanting to know what was going to happen around them in the near future. In other sexist discussions of the time, women were depicted as unable to control their emotions so would give away too much in their body language to fortune-tellers looking for cues for the information they would supply.

But none of this seemed to stop the people of Perth and Fremantle from going to have their fortunes told. Like other clients before them, the story went, Audrey and Cyril went along to a Fremantle 'palmist' who had been recommended to them. When they got there, she asked to read their palms. Audrey asked about their future wedding and the response was alarming: 'I can't see it ever taking place.' Looking over the lines that would foretell the future, the woman said there was a cloud between them that would end their relationship.

Unhappy with what she was hearing, Audrey took Cyril along to another fortune-teller. This time the prediction was even worse. Looking into crystal and sand, the person was startled by what they were seeing.

'I see blood in the crystal,' he told the young couple. 'It is between you.'

The fortune-teller added: 'You will never marry. It will be because of the blood. That's all.'

✦ ✦ ✦

Audrey hadn't wanted to go the ball in the first place. She had a terrible headache that morning and wasn't interested in being sociable. But Annie badly wanted her to. She did her best to convince Audrey they would have a great evening, and that they might meet some nice gentlemen. So Audrey gave in and turned up at the ball with Annie in their fancy dress costumes, hurrying past Sergeant Brodie into Government House.

Audrey seemed to have recovered from the ailments of the morning. The two young women danced happily for a short while before Audrey caught sight of Cyril Gidley dancing and laughing on the ballroom floor. It had been a few weeks since their relationship had ended and the engagement broken off, an event which had pleased Audrey's father. At the time, Audrey had seemed to take it quite well, speaking to her friends of 'sweet memories'.

Cyril was not meant to be there. Audrey was certain he was set to sail to Singapore that day on the *Kangaroo*. And now here he was, talking to a young woman at the entrance. He looked over in Audrey's direction and their eyes met, but Cyril looked straight through her, giving no sign of recognition.

Cyril Gidley's day had been a busy one. He had popped past the house of his friends, the Murphys, and then headed off on his motorbike to Fremantle to have his photograph professionally taken, looking dapper in his suit. He had caught up with a friend in Perth before turning up at the ball. He felt free to enjoy the evening, knowing he was on medical leave from work. He had only known his dancing partner for a short time, and he knew he needed to make a good impression because Maude Mitchell's mother was one of the organisers of the ball. The presence of Audrey at the ball was of little importance to him. But from Audrey's perspective, her former fiancé was giving her the cold shoulder. He continued to ignore her, even after passing Audrey and Annie on the dancefloor several times. After three hours of being ignored and watching her ex-lover 'taunt her', as Audrey saw it, she finally had enough and left the ball around midnight.

According to her testimony, she hurried back to her room in Surrey Chambers, where she partially undressed from her Pierrot costume and then, as she would later claim, 'sobbed for about half an

2. 'I SEE BLOOD BETWEEN YOU!'

hour'. Soon after this, she decided to put on a blue evening dress and go for a walk. And with her she took a revolver from the drawer next to her bed and wrapped it in a handkerchief.

The walk did little to calm Audrey. She wandered away from St Georges Terrace and the glistening lights of Government House, but found herself heading back there after a short while. She was thinking about Cyril. She just wanted to talk to him, for him at least to acknowledge her.

It was now close to one in the morning. At Government House, Sergeant Brodie's attentions were on guests leaving and making sure they departed promptly to avoid any noise complaints. He didn't see Audrey return in her blue evening gown. Nor did any of the other police officers. Even if they had, and had remembered Audrey had previously arrived in a fancy dress costume, her revolver was hidden under a white handkerchief.

Audrey headed inside and up to the balcony overlooking the dancefloor. Annie spotted her and hurried up to her there. She had to leave and needed the key to Audrey's room. Audrey told her where it was and, as they spoke, they saw Cyril talking to a young woman in the lounge area. Audrey asked her friend to tell Cyril that she wanted to speak to him. Annie agreed, anxious to get away and collect her things from Audrey's room in order to make the last charabanc in less than an hour.

Cyril moved to the dancefloor with Maude Mitchell. Annie had told him Audrey wanted to talk to him and as he spun his partner around, he saw Audrey up on the balcony. He carried on dancing.

Watching from above, Audrey took this as another dismissal. She descended the steps from the balcony and crossed the dancefloor. As she got closer to Cyril, he turned his back, still doing the foxtrot with Maude.

Audrey tapped him on the left shoulder. He turned around and said, 'Excuse me, I'm dancing.'

That was the final snub. The handkerchief fell from Audrey's hand and she pointed the revolver at Cyril. There was a single shot. Cyril's only reaction was his hand flying up to his forehead. Then he dropped to the floor.

From the vestibule, Constable John Wood heard the sound and ran to the ballroom. There, in the middle of the dancefloor, was Cyril. Someone called out, 'Look to the woman in blue.' He saw a young woman standing about a yard away from the wounded man, holding a revolver. Some witnesses would say that she had stood over the man's body shortly after firing.

Dr Sydney O'Neill heard the shot too and hurried to the injured man. He checked the pulse of the unmoving man. He saw blood coming out of the victim's mouth and felt a faint pulse.

'Move him to the cloakroom,' he told those close by, and together they carried Cyril there.

As the wounded man was laid down, Sydney lifted Cyril's shirt and underclothes and saw a small wound in the upper part of the chest. Blood and air were coming out of the bullet hole. By this stage, an ambulance had been called and it wouldn't be long before it had arrived at Government House.

Constable Alfred Timms was also now on his way to the ballroom from the back balcony. He took the stairs two at a time, and hurried through a side entrance. He saw the men carrying Cyril to the cloakroom and ran over to where a small crowd had gathered near a young woman.

Timms locked eyes with Wood and a look of concern passed between them. There could be no denying the woman had fired the revolver: it was still in her right hand. But where had she come from? Why had no one seen her with the weapon? And what had made her shoot the young man?

Audrey stood motionless, later recalling she felt as if she was in a 'form of complete unconsciousness'. Other guests would say she looked as if she was in a daze. PC Wood thought she looked 'cool and collected' and he took the revolver from her. For Wood, the young woman's elegant appearance jarred with his knowledge that she had just shot a man at close range.

'I did it,' Audrey told Constable Wood.

Wood saw something cold and distant about her as she looked beyond him to the chaos in the ballroom.

The revolver was given to one of the other police officers as evidence. By now the small crowd that had assembled included Sergeant Brodie. He had come running from outside when he heard what he later described as a sound like an electric light globe exploding, except that his police experience had told him it was a far more ominous sound. Sergeant Brodie pushed through the crowd, moving them on at the same time, and worried about protecting the crime scene. Despite the violent crimes he had seen on the job, he found it hard to believe that the young woman in front of him had committed this crime.

Then a young officer hurried over to tell him the victim had died in the cloakroom.

Brodie turned to Audrey. 'You are arrested on a charge of wilful murder.'

She remained silent while Constable Wood placed her under arrest and moved her away from the crowd. They would need to wait inside until the matron of the lock-up could be called and brought to Government House. She would need to be the one to escort the female prisoner away with the other police officers.

Sergeant Brodie went to the cloakroom and ordered Cyril Gidley's body to be removed to Perth Hospital Morgue. Maude Mitchell stood in shock as her dance partner's body was lifted onto a stretcher and taken away.

Then the matron arrived and Audrey Jacob was led from the ballroom, watched by the well-dressed crowd in silence.

3. '... to keep her own counsel'

Even though it was standard procedure, Detective Sergeant Joseph Frazer walked into the police lock-up feeling uncomfortable. He was there to check on a young woman accused of wilful murder. Frazer had prosecuted his fair share of women in his many years of policing but mainly for drunkenness, soliciting and vagrancy. There was Esther Warden, for one, who was known as the 'terror of the West End' of Fremantle. She gave officers a run for their money across the metropolitan centre, that was for sure, in her agitated and drunken state. Such offences against good order were far more common than a murder charge. And it was even more rare to see a fresh-faced young murderer in an evening gown.

Joseph Frazer hadn't been at the ball the evening before. He was in bed at home when he was called out at three in the morning to join the police investigation. He tried not to waken his wife, Ella, and was grateful they didn't still have four little kids at home. When they were very little, he would try and sneak out for a job only to return home to find Ella had been awake with them all after he left.

At seven thirty on the morning of 27 August, only six hours after Cyril Gidley was fatally shot, DS Frazer walked along the corridor to the cell where Audrey Jacob was sitting on the bed, in quiet repose, still in her attire from the night before. Frazer was still trying to get it straight in his own head how this had all happened.

3. '... TO KEEP HER COUNSEL'

'Do you desire to tell me anything about the affair at Government House Ballroom?' he asked her.

She didn't answer him, but stared straight ahead, avoiding eye contact. DS Frazer told her that she was formally charged with wilful murder and cautioned her, 'You need not say anything but if you do say anything it could be used against you in a court of law.'

'I do not desire to make any statement,' Audrey replied.

DS Frazer returned a short while later with clothing that he had taken from Audrey's room at Surrey Chambers. He hadn't needed the landlady to give him access, though she had been there to watch, as he had the key taken from Audrey's friend, Annie, as she waited for the last charabanc to Fremantle. Out of sight, Audrey changed out of her blue evening dress and it was given to Frazer. He bagged and marked it as evidence while chatter continued in the station around him about the young woman now awaiting a court appearance.

On a bright, cool Thursday August morning, the people of Perth were waking up to the shocking news. The ballroom shooting story ran across all the newspapers and even featured in national publications, and the city was captivated.

Hours after the shooting, the *Daily News* included a brief mention of the tragedy on its front page but encouraged its readers to flip to page ten for further details of the 'highly sensational circumstances' of the shooting. Reporters had worked hard to establish brief background details for Audrey and Cyril and had tracked down eyewitnesses able to recall the young art student who calmly stood and shot a man on the dancefloor.

Reporters were also there for Audrey's first appearance in the Perth Police Court on a charge of wilful murder. The press reported that she seemed 'undisturbed and unemotional' and was 'tall and of attractive appearance'. Accompanying her was one of Perth's most successful lawyers, Arthur Goodwin Haynes. He had been given instructions to defend the murder charge and moved quickly to be able to represent Audrey as best he could.

Arthur Haynes had represented a lot of women in his time as a lawyer, from petty offenders to brothel madams and their workers from the red-light district on Roe Street, Perth. He was already a well-known criminal lawyer, following in his father's footsteps. Richard Haynes had arrived with his wife, Marion, in Western Australia in 1885. He had been admitted to the New South Wales Bar in 1880 and set up a legal firm on St Georges Terrace, Perth. There were eleven children in the Haynes family—Arthur being the second oldest—and things didn't slow down for his father. Richard Haynes became Kings Counsel in 1902, after briefly serving as mayor for North Perth. When Marion died suddenly before her forty-first birthday in 1905, nineteen-year-old Arthur Haynes took up legal work to help out around the house. His father remarried in 1908 but there were no more siblings. By the 1920s, Arthur was a well-known criminal lawyer but his father would not live to see him represent Audrey Jacob. Richard Haynes died in 1922 and was deeply mourned by the Perth community, especially those in the legal profession who recognised his commitment to social justice:

> No other member of the profession had so endeared himself by qualities of heart and soul to help fellow professionals as had Mr. Haynes. If he had one characteristic which was more lovable and deserving of approbation than any other it was his invariable willingness to extend a helping hand to the man who fell by the roadside or was in any sort of misfortune or trouble. Mr. Haynes was the man to whom the unfortunate and oppressed always looked for help and sympathy, which was never refused.

Arthur Haynes was cut from the same cloth as his father. As legal practitioners they were both committed to doing their best to represent people from across society, and were particularly drawn to helping the more disadvantaged. Arthur, however, was also keen to take on cases that would bring him interest from the media and make him a high-profile legal practitioner in Perth.

When Arthur Haynes learned about the shooting at Government House and that it was a young woman who had fired the fatal shot, he sprang into action. He spent much of 27 August setting up his brief

3. '... TO KEEP HER COUNSEL'

to defend Audrey Jacob. While other lawyers might have avoided such a case, given the clear evidence Audrey had shot Cyril Gidley, Haynes saw an opportunity. Over the course of an hour and a half that Thursday morning, he talked at length with Audrey about what had happened. He also travelled down to Fremantle to meet with Audrey's parents only to find that they had travelled up to Perth.

In the Police Court that morning, Audrey Jacob was less concerned with her lawyer's impressive legal brief than she was with setting out how she was to be treated. She told Arthur Haynes to instruct the police magistrate, Alfred Kidson, the same man who would serve as district coroner at the upcoming inquest, that she didn't want any more visits from the detectives. She was refusing to make a statement, instead wanting, in her lawyer's words, 'to keep her own counsel'.

The inquest was set to begin on 3 September. Audrey was remanded for eight days and sent to Fremantle Prison.

It was obvious to Arthur Haynes that Audrey was putting up a tough front in order to cope with her incarceration but he wondered just what was going through her mind. Why had she shot Cyril Gidley? What had transpired between the pair to lead to this? Arthur Haynes planned to spend the next few days preparing Audrey for the inquest, watching and listening closely to her, and establishing how best to represent her as the accused and to determine a strategy to defend her when, ultimately, the case went to trial, as of course, it must.

Earlier that morning, as Audrey was taken into custody and then appeared in court, Cyril Gidley's body was taken to Perth Hospital and placed in the morgue. Detective Sergeant Joseph Frazer made enquiries for a formal identification. With his family overseas and interstate, Cyril's friends Edward Cutting and William Murphy were asked to identify his body. Edward Cutting was also an engineer. He and his wife lived in a worker's cottage on Forrest Street, East Fremantle. In the months to come, Edward would liaise with the police to get Cyril's estate settled and his belongings sent back to his family.

Matthew Waddell, an orderly at the hospital, took charge of the body, stripped it, and gave the clothes to DS Frazer. Though he had done this many times before, some cases were worse than others. Cyril Gidley was a young man cut down in his prime, and his personal effects had meaning to people who knew and loved him. Now he lay cold and lifeless upon the gurney. Death in the mortuary made Matthew Waddell appreciate life even more.

The chief medical officer, forty-one-year-old Donald Stuart MacKenzie, conducted the post-mortem. He was a likeable, professional man well known about Perth Hospital for his genuine care for patients, particularly those with mental health issues who often suffered being placed in the lock-up while the police worked out what to do with them. It was Dr MacKenzie who would be brought in to assess them.

The last few weeks had been particularly hard for Donald MacKenzie. He was working long hours at the hospital and worrying about care for his three young children. His beloved wife, Margaret Daisy, had died on 4 June, aged forty-two. The local community rallied around him but it couldn't take away the emptiness of the family home, and John, Rosalind and Diana missing their mother. Donald was distracted from this, however, on 27 August as he prepared to make his own contribution to one of the city's most extraordinary cases.

Cyril Gidley's naked body lay on the grey mortuary stretcher. His dinner suit, silver wristwatch, driver's licence, white gloves and white handkerchief had all been bagged as evidence for the police.

Donald MacKenzie was assisted by the orderly to place Cyril's body on the medical table. The doctor started jotting down the details of the post-mortem for his report to the coroner. The cause of death was obvious. There was a gunshot wound in the chest where a bullet was found beneath the skin, on the right side. There were signs on the right lower abdomen of an earlier operation and MacKenzie put this down as having occurred around six months beforehand. The wound indicated that the shot had been inflicted at close range—otherwise, it would have gone through the body.

Dr MacKenzie had the medical experience to back this judgement but he had also seen many bullet and shrapnel wounds. He had enlisted with the Australian Infantry Force in August 1914 and was appointed captain and then promoted to major for his commendations working in the 2nd Australian General Hospital in Egypt and France. His six years of study at the University of Sydney were to prepare him for the worst of what he might see in a hospital but it paled in comparison to frontline casualties during the war.

Blood was 'exuding' from the mouth and nose and MacKenzie noted both were also full of blood clot. On closer inspection of the chest wound, the doctor found that the bullet had entered into the left side between the fourth and fifth ribs and lodged in the right side between the fifth and sixth ribs. It was removed from here during the post-mortem. There was a 'through and through puncture of descending aorta' and both lungs were perforated.

Donald MacKenzie ruled that death was from a 'haemorrhage following gun shot wound of chest'. The bullet, a twenty-five calibre, was removed from the right side of the chest and bagged as evidence.

Cyril Gidley was stitched back up, his body covered, and placed on the stretcher. He was once again taken on the lonely, quiet trip back to the refrigerated cabinet where his body would be held until his funeral.

There were no surprises in Dr MacKenzie's port-mortem report for Arthur Haynes. Cyril Gidley had been shot in the chest at close range in front of several witnesses, and it was Haynes' client who had shot him. While he put together his brief, Haynes began to conceive of a plan for gaining sympathy for Audrey. He would secure the help of the press. He knew that the *Daily News* would be less interested in hearing out Haynes' pleas for some sympathy for the accused. On the morning of the shooting it had written up a short piece on Cyril Gidley, calling him a 'likeable Englishman'.

The *Mirror* newspaper editor, Victor Courtney, was the centrepiece of Haynes' plans. The fact Courtney had been at the ball and saw the shooting and its aftermath unfold, meant he was especially interested in the case but Arthur needed to manipulate the press so that he could have a chance of controlling some of the story that would get out to the public.

The day after he appeared in the Police Court with Audrey Jacob, Arthur Haynes did the rounds of the main newspaper offices in Perth. He marched in to the editors of the *West Australian* demanding they retract a report from earlier that day which had claimed Audrey and Cyril had argued on the day of the dance. Haynes insisted that his client had not seen her ex-fiancé before the ball and had in fact expected him to have been working away on the *Kangaroo*. It was partly the shock of seeing him at the ball and dancing with other women which had driven her to snap.

Arthur Haynes' visit to Victor Courtney at his *Mirror* newspaper office in Murray Street was more positive. He knew Victor well and frequently stopped by the newspaper building for work. Arthur Haynes was often paid to look over newspaper copy for libel and in turn he would share information from his work at the courts. Though he was friendly with John Joseph 'Jack' Simons, the paper's other owner, Arthur and Victor had more of a rapport.

Victor Courtney was happy to see his lawyer friend this Friday 28 August because he knew Arthur was representing Audrey Jacob. Victor liked a 'good murder', as he would say, because it increased his newspaper's circulation. He had learned the newspaper trade from his father, who had worked in country papers, first in New South Wales and then in Greenbushes in the south-west of Western Australia. Henry Courtney had started up the *Greenbushes Advocate* in 1899 and put in the hard yards. This meant he found the news, wrote editorials, and set the type. The paper was also staunchly independent and Henry Courtney was often outspoken, something that didn't go unnoticed in a country town. Three years after it started, the newspaper folded. Though the Greenbushes gamble had not paid off for his father, Victor Courtney admired his father's hard work and took up journalism. He worked at the *Sunday Times*, bought the *WA Sportsman* with his friend Jack Simons, left the *Sunday Times* and changed the name of their newspaper to the *Call*. But the pair didn't want to be small newspaper

3. '... TO KEEP HER COUNSEL'

proprietors. The *Mirror* opened on 1 April 1922 and two years later really took off with a shocking murder case featuring Arthur Haynes.

The 'good murder' hit the newspapers when a body was found floating in Crawley Bay. The police were called and the reporters descended on Nedlands Police Station, keen to know who the person was and if foul play was suspected. Nineteen-year-old Frank Davidson, one of the *Mirror*'s new journalists, wrote the reports that would captivate the city. The body in the bay was taxi driver John O'Neill who, police would allege, had been murdered by George Auburn. Mr Auburn had come to the attention of officers when he reported having found O'Neill's coat on the night of the murder. Then he said he had come across blood and hair when checking out a motorbike on Westana Road, Dalkeith (which was renamed Waratah Avenue after the murder and trial). The police were even more suspicious when one of Auburn's buttons was found in the taxi driver's blood-splattered car, which had been dumped in Leederville. The Crown Prosecution case was being made by Hubert Parker and Arthur Haynes, in a trial that lasted twenty days. Auburn was found guilty but mercy was recommended on the basis of his youth—he was twenty-four—and he would be saved a hanging but serve twenty years in prison. That murder story boosted the *Mirror*'s circulation to ten thousand.

And now, a little over a year later, Arthur Haynes was in Victor Courtney's office with another murder case to share. This time he was on the other side of the legal table defending an even younger accused, a young woman whom Haynes knew the *Mirror* would be especially interested in and might just help his case.

By the weekend, Arthur's visit to Victor was paying off. The newspaper was able to establish the main details of the shooting for the public. 'BALLROOM HORROR!', the front page headline of the *Mirror* declared. In the flowery language the paper was known for, it set out the drama of what unfolded:

> PERTH'S greatest ballroom shone brilliant with light and gaiety on Wednesday night, when hundreds of glad-hearted boys and girls and their elders danced and made merry to aid the benevolence of the Hospital of St. John of God.

They had 'chased the glowing hours with flying feet,' and the grand ball was drawing to a happy close, the night had passed into early morn.

It was one of those scenes on which the High Gods seem to smile.

Then a shot, hushed chatter, little startled cries, a scatter of dancers, a girl with a revolver, and a young man, with a blood smeared face, dying on the floor.

The High Gods had deserted their chosen. Terror was upon the gay hall. Mirth fled away into the shadows.

The glory of the lights and the gaiety of the colors, the music and the laughter, gave way to the awe that betokened the presence of the Dreadful Great.

King Death had entered in!

The story stretched across the front page and onto page two, with profile photographs of Audrey Jacob, Cyril Gidley and Arthur Haynes. This was a popular practice employed by the *Mirror* to gain more readers but these private photographs of Audrey and Cyril were carefully positioned, and in a way that Arthur Haynes would like. Cyril was standing in side profile with a cigarette in his mouth and a hat on, looking a little older than his twenty-five years. Audrey's photograph at the top left of the article was there to grab the interest of the public. She appeared younger than her twenty years and was looking over her shoulder and smiling serenely at readers. If Arthur was reading things well, these kinds of stories would go a long way to building a sympathetic public connection to Audrey.

Cyril Gidley's funeral was held on the afternoon of Friday 28 August. His distraught parents, brother and sister, thousands of miles away in England, were unable to attend so it fell to the people who had known him in Perth and family friends to organise the proceedings.

3. '... TO KEEP HER COUNSEL'

The funeral ceremony was conducted by Reverend G.R. Holland. The cortege moved from the Bowra and O'Dea private mortuary building on Pier Street, Perth to the Church of England section of Karrakatta Cemetery. Maude Mitchell, Cyril's friend and dance partner the evening he was shot, was there at the funeral along with other friends of Cyril's, some she knew and others who were more his work crowd. She had suffered a great deal in the hours after the ball. She was bothered by the thoughts of what might have been if she could have just turned Cyril around in the dance. But no one had been prepared for a young woman armed with a revolver held at point-blank range.

Maude Michell's father served as one of the pallbearers. He had come to know Cyril well enough on his recent medical visits and had grown to like him. The other pallbearers also included Edward Cutting and some of Cyril's workmates. Twenty wreaths from friends and workmates were laid out on the grave but there was one in particular that caught the attention of the mourners.

Earlier in the day, Audrey Jacob told her lawyer she wanted to send a wreath to the funeral. Not wanting people to know that it was from her, she had requested an anonymous card to be included. Arthur Haynes organised it and so, there with the other wreaths, was the one from the woman who had killed Cyril. The note read: 'From one who will never forget.'

4. 'The Remarkable Eyes of Audrey Campbell Jacob'

The inquest opened at 10.00 am on Thursday 3 September, one week after Cyril Gidley's death. The press was at the ready outside of the Perth Courthouse, along with a few keen spectators and some of Audrey's supporters, including family and friends.

There had been a fair amount of speculation about the witnesses and twenty were expected to appear, including Audrey's parents. Edward and Jessie Jacob walked to the courthouse together, trying to avoid questions from the reporters. Jessie wore a long jacket over her blouse and long skirt; she kept her eyes low, and clutched her handbag close. Edward Jacob was dressed in a suit, tie and hat and was photographed looking straight at the camera, a slight hint of a smile on his lips.

But it was Audrey the reporters wanted to see. She was in the custody of Helen Dugdale of the Women Police and they were travelling together by motor car from Fremantle Prison. Helen Dugdale had supervised many young women over the years but they were usually runaways and streetwalkers, not a twenty-year-old accused of wilful murder.

Audrey Jacob didn't disappoint. She stepped out of the car and walked up to the court building dressed in a silk navy-blue dress covered over with a henna-coloured overcoat with fur cuffs. On her

4. 'THE REMARKABLE EYES OF AUDREY CAMPBELL JACOB'

head she wore a cloche hat with floral decorations. Whisked quickly into the courtroom, she sat next to her counsel, Arthur Haynes, glancing occasionally over at her parents.

Arthur Haynes was known as a self-assured, opportunistic lawyer but today his entrance was less confident than he had hoped. He hobbled into the room, aided by crutches, clearly in pain from a recent car accident. But Arthur Haynes was always looking for the best legal angle. Right now he looked like a struggling lawyer in need of sympathy. When he rose a short while later to begin his opening address, Haynes was shaky on his feet. It was perfect.

Alfred Bowman Kidson, the acting police magistrate overseeing the coronial inquest, looked out at the courtroom, observing Audrey and her lawyer and the police prosecutor, Detective Sergeant Joseph Frazer. Sixty-one-year-old Alfred Kidson was born in Paddington, England, had been admitted to the West Australian Bar in 1887 and practised law out in the country, at Northam, one hundred kilometres east of Perth, before moving back to the city. He had been a Member of the Legislative Council from 1895 until 1902. Kidson was known to wear a flower in his suit jacket buttonhole as he presided over coronial inquests, his glasses often perched on the end of his nose as he carefully listened and wrote down evidence given before him. He was a likeable man, frequently seen pottering about in the front garden of his house on Adelaide Terrace, and affectionately referred to as 'A.B.'. He was also well respected for his knowledge of the law and fair dispensation of it. Now he was responsible for determining if the shooting of Cyril Gidley was wilful murder and should proceed to trial.

Kidson knew that DS Frazer and his officers would have worked hard to ensure that all the main witnesses for the police case were present at the inquest. Some would be able to establish what happened on the dancefloor while others had known Cyril Gidley and could shed some light on his relationship with Audrey. Kidson also knew that Audrey's lawyer would be doing his bit to evoke as much sympathy as possible for his client. Kidson was a professional. It was the evidence that would decide Audrey's fate. It was hard, though, to see how, on the facts, it could not be straightforward.

Jessie Jacob was the first witness called. Led in her deposition by Audrey's lawyer and questioned by the police prosecutor, Jessie spoke of a family in turmoil but not because of Audrey's actions at the ball. She claimed they were the victims of Cyril Gidley's crusade to tear the family apart and control Audrey.

Audrey, her mother outlined, had been educated at the Roman Catholic Convent in Norseman until she was sixteen and it was there that she had taken up painting. She kept it up afterwards and sold some of her works to people in the Eastern States. Jessie first met Cyril in June 1924 when he came to the family home with Audrey.

'From the very first he made bad accusations against my husband about women,' Jessie revealed, embarrassed to be sharing this in court and with her husband seated nearby. She told the room that Edward denied seeing other women but tensions increased in the house. Edward moved out in August and went to stay at a boarding house nearby run by an Allan Spence.

Cyril Gidley was intent on keeping Edward Jacob out of the house. Jessie told the court that he booked into the boarding house under an alias, Cyril Douglas, and planned to spy on Edward and report back to Jessie. He wanted to gather damning information about Jessie's husband so he could use it against Edward to prevent him from opposing Cyril's relationship with Audrey. It was clear to Cyril that Edward Jacob did not want him seeing his daughter.

By October 1924, Jessie explained, Audrey was engaged to Cyril. She showed her mother a sapphire ring and seemed very happy. It wasn't long before Edward Jacob found out about the engagement, which would be announced in the newspapers soon after.

In the meantime, Cyril had other plans for the Jacobs' house while Edward was living away. During his visits to see Audrey he told Jessie that he wanted to add two rooms to her family's house. He would pay for this if Jessie handled the title deeds over to him. One of the rooms would be used to store 'smuggled goods from Singapore' he had hidden on the *Kangaroo*.

'He said he had done a lot of smuggling', Jessie explained from the witness stand, and had got into 'a lot of scrapes at home' before his father 'turned him out for five years'.

4. 'THE REMARKABLE EYES OF AUDREY CAMPBELL JACOB'

He pleaded with Jessie that Audrey was the only person who could save him and when they got married, he planned to take her 'home to his people'.

Jessie Jacob was not intimidated. She wanted nothing to do with Cyril's plan, even when he threatened Audrey and, according to Jessie, said he would 'kill her if she threw him over'.

Jessie went to her husband to tell him about the smuggling plans. He convinced her they had to tell the police. Detective Sergeant Cowie at Fremantle Station was informed and warrants were issued to look for smuggled goods on the *Kangaroo*. The detectives seized some stolen goods but Cyril boasted to Jessie afterwards that they hadn't been able to pin it on him and they also didn't turn up all the goods.

Two days later, on 8 October, Audrey and Cyril's engagement was officially announced in the newspapers. Edward Jacob, as unhappy as he might have been, could do little to oppose it. He had been temporarily transferred to Katanning as an assistant clerk of court. Jessie claimed Cyril was doing his best not to let Edward back in the house and had been in touch with people in Katanning seeing if the appointment could be made permanent. When Edward returned not long after, Cyril was told in no uncertain terms he would have to see Audrey 'away from home'.

It became even more complicated when Audrey moved to Perth on 11 November 1924. Cyril wrote threatening letters to Jessie, wanting to see Audrey and upset that her family would keep her from him. He claimed he had not known that Audrey moved out of home. But according to Jessie Jacob, Cyril had been in her house when Audrey was packing to leave. Cyril continued to make threats against Edward Jacob, even bringing Jessie to the point of removing one of her daughters out of school amid the threats.

Then he became even more domineering and harsh towards Audrey. She told her mother that Cyril had demanded she return home. He couldn't be engaged to a girl living away from home, claiming the Freemasons would not approve. He would have to end the engagement. Audrey moved back home a fortnight after she had left.

Then there were the threatening letters with lies about the family and how Audrey was being treated. One of them, reproduced in the

Mirror newspaper, was said to have been written by Cyril Gidley to Jessie Jacob on 14 November. This was when Audrey had moved out and Cyril claimed he had not been told. It read:

> Mrs. Jacob.—
> It may and it may not interest you to know that I have at last found Audrey, and she told me the reason she left home. She left unknown to me, although I saw her the same day. It is not my way to threaten, for which I am not going to, but unless Audrey is treated with more respect before I sail again, I shall make it my duty to tell your brother, Mr. Junner, in Perth, all that I know, also about your husband homecoming, and I do not think that that would be very nice.
>
> I am sorry to write this, but my believe is that Audrey had not had a fair go, and as to half feeding the girl, well that is not very motherlike. I will give you till next Tuesday to think well what I have said; if by then you still wish to treat your daughter so, I shall carry out my intentions. If I am standing in the way, meaning the friendship which exists between Audrey and myself, we will leave it to her to decide.
>
> I am confident that there is a grievance somewhere. Audrey has been very good to you, and this is what she gets in return. The reward is very shallow for what she did for you a few weeks back. Don't forget that please.
>
> Well, trusting you will think well before being definite, I will not go into affairs any further.
>   C. GIDLEY.

There was more, however, to Audrey having moved out, according to her mother. Audrey returned home at 11 pm on 9 November after an evening with Cyril at Mrs Murphy's place, where he was staying. Jessie waited up for her daughter and when she came in she was not her usual smiling and happy self. She went straight to her bedroom. Jessie went in and found Audrey sobbing but she wouldn't talk to her.

'She had a sort of clutch mark on her shoulder.'

4. 'THE REMARKABLE EYES OF AUDREY CAMPBELL JACOB'

The next day, 'some blood attracted' Jessie's attention. She did not reveal where it was but Audrey dismissed her mother's worries.

Jessie told the courtroom: 'She has never been the same girl since. She has been moody.'

Despite this, Jessie continued to make appointments for Audrey and Cyril to meet away from the house. Her husband didn't know about these arranged meetings.

When questioned by the police prosecutor DS Frazer, Jessie confirmed that Audrey had a revolver. This had been given to her by an ex-fiancé, Claude Arundel, who was third officer on the *Bendigo*. Arundel had given the gun to Audrey as a present so she had protection. Their engagement had been broken when Audrey met Cyril Gidley.

The prosecutor asked if this was the same revolver which was used to shoot Cyril Gidley.

Jessie said it was.

Detective Sergeant Frazer made a note of the prior engagement to Claude Arundel. He had to be careful not to focus on the morals of Audrey in the upcoming trial, because the judge could well take issue with this, but this detail could be important. Audrey had been engaged when she met Cyril. She had broken off this engagement and yet when Cyril had done the same, Audrey had lashed out, fatally. Joseph Frazer didn't know if anything could be made of this but it was interesting all the same.

Audrey moved to the city a few weeks before the ballroom shooting to continue her studies at the Perth Technical School. Cyril had now taken to riding his motorbike up and down the street near the Jacob house in Fremantle, including the day he died. Jessie thought his actions were dangerous.

Audrey Jacob wrote to her mother on 17 August 1925 asking for her to send the revolver. She said that her room in Surrey Chambers had been broken into and her diary stolen. Jessie told the courtroom she thought Cyril was away on the *Kangaroo* and sent the revolver so that 'my daughter could not have got the revolver to use on him'.

As a police prosecutor, these words would strike Joseph Frazer as almost damning. Audrey's own mother had thought she might use the revolver on Cyril Gidley. Audrey's lawyer saw it another way. Cyril

Gidley had been terrorising the Jacob family. He could have pushed any of them to breaking point. Was this a defence for Audrey's actions at the ball? It certainly could be used to win over a jury in a trial.

Edward Jacob was the next witness called. Now an assistant clerk of courts at Fremantle, he confirmed his marital problems: 'Sometime last year disputes arose between my wife and I resulting in me leaving home.' Like Jessie, he believed this was made worse when Cyril Gidley started seeing Audrey. When he met Cyril at the boarding house, Edward quickly worked out who he was, even with him using the alias. He told the courtroom, 'He was trying to break up my home.'

Edward recalled confronting Cyril on the street about it.

'What is your game in trying to separate my wife from me?' he asked.

Cyril seemed to enjoy the attention and upsetting Audrey's father.

Edward told him there was no truth in the accusations and Cyril knew this 'perfectly well'. He wanted Cyril to fix it.

'I can do lots of things if I like,' Cyril replied. 'Audrey is going to be my wife and there's nothing you can do about it.'

Edward Jacob also told Detective Sergeant Cowie at Fremantle Station about the way Cyril was treating him so 'that if anything happened to me he would know who had done it.'

Unlike his wife, Edward Jacob's statement was a lot shorter. Was Audrey's lawyer worried that her father might say something that would further implicate her? DS Frazer wondered at his usefulness as a witness ultimately to the defence in a trial.

Detective Sergeant Frazer was concerned, however, after only two witnesses being called, that Arthur Haynes was creating a sympathetic case for Audrey and tarnishing the victim's reputation.

The inquest was adjourned to Monday 7 September. Audrey was remanded for a further eight days and taken back to Fremantle Prison. Edward and Jessie Jacob returned home to their other children with the sinking knowledge that their private troubles were now going to be public knowledge. But they had to do what they could to help Audrey. Her lawyer was certainly upfront about what was needed to give Audrey the slightest chance of being able to have a convincing defence.

4. 'THE REMARKABLE EYES OF AUDREY CAMPBELL JACOB'

✦ ✦ ✦

The Saturday evening edition of the *Mirror* newspaper was where Victor Courtney would grab readers with shocking stories. And now he had one of the best to sell papers over the weekend. Courtney was following the Cyril Gidley inquest and jotting down key details for a striking front-page story that he hoped would sell many copies.

Audrey was important to raking in more sales. Courtney developed the story around the main headline: 'INQUEST OPENS In Ballroom Tragedy, Parents' Sensational Stories'. Photographs were positioned to capture more interest and the most prominent was of Audrey walking demurely into the inquest. There was no over-the-shoulder smile this time. Her parents had been through a 'trying ordeal' in giving evidence at the first day of proceedings. Jessie Jacob, the *Mirror* reported, had fainted on her way to the court and the full strain of what she was going through was obvious. The *Mirror*'s campaign to gather sympathy for Audrey was fully underway.

Readers turning over the page were then taken almost into the world of F. Scott Fitzgerald's *The Great Gatsby*. Only a few months before, the novel had been released featuring artwork by a Spanish artist which he had called 'celestial eyes'. Fitzgerald loved the work and wanted it on the cover to represent his main female protagonist, Daisy Buchanan's eyes. Daisy was the captivating love interest of Jay Gatsby in the story and ultimately brought about his undoing. And now, the *Mirror* cropped a photograph of Audrey Jacob to show only her eyes under the headline: 'THE REMARKABLE EYES OF AUDREY CAMPBELL JACOB'. It wasn't far off being a local nod to *The Great Gatsby* and this real-life story certainly had the drama.

Audrey's eyes, the story went, had been 'discussed by every observer'. When she looked up in court, her eyes 'attracted everybody's gaze'. They were striking but also spoke of something deeper in the young woman:

> They are the eyes of one whose thoughts are really not with the immediate things around them. There is about

them the mistiness that is not brought by tears, but it is associated almost with the dreamer.

She does not look at you. She looks through you, beyond you, away somewhere in the distance as it were.

...

They are the eyes that suggest
ARTISTRY AND INTELLECT
and the habits of one who thinks too much.

The *Mirror* story then made the claim that Audrey's character could be determined from her eyes: 'Students of psychology place much value on the eye as an expression of character'. And then came the bold statement: 'They are remarkable, the eyes of this twenty-year-old girl, the most remarkable I think that I have ever seen in or out of the court'.

Arthur Haynes couldn't have played it any better had he tried. There was little mention of the ex-lover whom Audrey had shot dead on the dancefloor. Instead, she was presented to all of Perth as a daydreamer, an artistic and creative young woman who was in court because of the actions of her abusive ex-partner.

5. 'She appeared to be in a dazed condition'

The inquest reopened on Monday 7 September with nine key witnesses called to give evidence by the police prosecution. The first was Sydney O'Neill, the Perth doctor who had been at the ball and witnessed the aftermath of the shooting. O'Neill recounted he had been dancing on the ballroom floor when he heard a shot, turned around and saw Cyril lying on the floor about two yards from him. He rushed over, took Cyril's pulse and then carried him with others to the cloakroom. Cyril was still alive but unconscious and O'Neill knew the blood and air coming out of his mouth and nostrils was a bad sign. He quickly turned up Cyril's shirt and saw the bullet wound in the chest. A minute later, Cyril was dead.

Donald MacKenzie was called next and confirmed his post-mortem report which was entered as 'Exhibit D'. Cyril Gidley had been shot at close range and the bullet to his lung and heart was fatal. When cross-examined by Arthur Haynes, he revealed another startling aspect of the case. Had Audrey Jacob stepped back 'two or three paces', the bullet would not have lodged in Cyril Gidley's chest. Its velocity would have meant it could have continued through his body and hit someone else. It was a reminder that the scene could have been even worse.

Police evidence was critical to the inquest and so on this second day of proceedings, three key police officers were called to give evidence. Arthur Haynes was particularly keen to hear what they had to say. Knowing the inquest would most likely lead to a trial, he was looking for anything that might cast doubt over police actions following the shooting.

Police Constable John Wood and Sergeant William Brodie gave evidence. Wood was on duty in the vestibule of the ballroom when at 1.30 am he 'heard a shot fired as if from a revolver in the Ballroom'. He ran into the ballroom and found that there was still a dance in progress. He looked over at the centre of the dancefloor and saw a man lying on the floor.

Sergeant Brodie was at the entrance of the vestibule when he heard was sounded like 'the explosion of an electric light globe'. As he entered the ballroom, a man told him that a man had been shot. At that point, Constable Wood was walking a young woman over to him.

Constable Wood had gone straight over to Audrey when he caught sight of the scene in the middle of the ballroom. He took her by the left arm and noticed that she was holding a revolver in her right hand. She said to him, 'I did it.' Wood took possession of the gun and Audrey asked him to take her away.

It was now that he passed Sergeant Brodie on the dancefloor, as he was taking Audrey over to place her behind one of the pillars to sit her down on a chair. He told Brodie, 'This is the girl that fired the shot.'

The young woman didn't say anything to Brodie and he returned his attention to the man on the floor. There was blood oozing from his mouth and nose and he was quickly taken to the cloakroom. When Cyril died only minutes later, Brodie went back to Wood and Audrey. He asked Audrey how long she had known the shot man and she said it had been about two and a half years. This evidence was not interrogated, however, which is odd, given all other evidence pointed to Audrey having known Cyril for a year.

Arthur Haynes was not happy with how this line of questioning had unfolded. He asked Constable Wood if, in his experience, it was true that often people did not show outward signs of strain. Wood agreed but when questioned about this handling of the revolver, he defended his actions, saying that he had given it to Sergeant Frazer

5. 'SHE APPEARED TO BE IN A DAZED CONDITION'

who had then examined it in his presence and found it to be loaded and cocked. The empty cartridge had also been found and Wood had given it to Sergeant Brodie.

Wood told the inquest that he had had a conversation with Audrey while they waited at the pillar.

'What did you do a thing like that for?' Wood asked Audrey.

Audrey stared straight ahead. 'I prefer not to say anything now. It will come out after all.'

When Sergeant Brodie came over, Audrey asked if the man was dead.

'Yes, he only lasted four or five minutes,' Brodie told her.

The coldness descended again across Audrey's face: 'He only got what he deserved, and everybody that knows him will say the same.'

Alfred Timms also gave evidence. Like his colleague, William Brodie, Alfred was originally from Victoria. He moved to Western Australia in 1897 and worked as a shunter at the Midland Railway Company before later following his trade as a blacksmith. He was an accomplished pianist, organist and band instrument player and when he joined the police force in 1902, he was able to keep up his musical interests in the Police Band. The Audrey Jacob case would go down as one of the most significant in his career and he had been there to see it all unfold at Government House.

Police officer Alfred George Timms had been standing at the foot of the staircase of the back balcony when he heard a 'report' coming from the ballroom. He hurried towards the sound and saw Cyril Gidley being carried out of the cloakroom and Constable Wood on the other side of the room with Audrey Jacob.

Alfred Timms explained at the inquest that Audrey had told him she had her reasons for shooting Cyril Gidley.

'They must be serious to justify this.'

'I gave him plenty of warning,' Audrey replied, 'but he took no notice.'

Arthur Haynes listened closely to what the police were saying and wanted to cast some doubt over their handling of Audrey and the scene. A testy cross-examination followed with Alfred Timms.

Haynes asked: 'Was there an arrangement between the police that they should attempt to "pump" this girl in turn?'

'None whatever,' Timms replied. 'I was only the second constable to speak to her.'

Haynes continued. 'Do you know that, owing to the condition she felt herself in, she had already refused to answer questions?'

'I don't think she had.'

'She had. She had told Constable Wood.'

'That was a quarter of an hour after I had spoken to her.'

'She was under arrest?'

'Yes.'

'You did not caution her?'

'No. I did not think it was necessary to do so.'

Arthur Haynes showed the courtroom his surprised look. 'Why? Because it was only a murder charge? Has it not been laid down time and time again that it is the duty of the police to warn people before asking them questions?'

Alfred Timms was trying not to waver and allow any show that Haynes was getting to him. 'Yes.'

'Yet you departed from your known course of duty?'

'I had not arrested her. She was merely left in my charge.'

Haynes persisted, given Timms had just said she was under arrest. 'You knew that anything she might say could be used against her, yet you deliberately refrained from warning her?'

'No.'

'I suppose you considered it quite fair in the case of a person placed in the position in which this girl finds herself?'

'I think it is perfectly fair to speak the truth when you are in the witness box.'

'Do you consider it fair to question a girl regarding incidents in connection with which she was charged with murder, within a few minutes of the shot being fired?'

'Yes. I think I was justified. I did it on the spur of the moment.'

'Do you know that, despite her announcement that she did not want to make a statement, she was plied with questions that night, and that she was wakened in the morning so that she could be questioned by several other persons?'

5. 'SHE APPEARED TO BE IN A DAZED CONDITION'

'I do not.'

'In other words, they would not take "No" for an answer.'

Constable Timms did well under pressure, and the exchange ended with him telling Haynes, 'I know nothing about that.'

Alfred Timms left the witness box and would later confer with his colleagues. The police version of events and their initial impressions of Audrey were different to the picture her lawyer was trying to convey about what had happened that evening. Arthur Haynes was bringing attention to the actions of the police, and their following of police procedure, in what could be a prelude to a trial defence and efforts to gain sympathy for the accused.

The next witness was Annie Humphreys. Her appearance in the lower court was long anticipated. As Audrey's friend and the person who accompanied her to the ball, she could provide some insights into exactly what happened on the evening of the shooting. As they had done with Audrey's parents, the newspaper photographers and reporters were waiting for her. Annie wore a long, flapper-styled dress, a string of pearls and a cloche hat pulled down to just above her eyebrows. *Truth* newspaper ran a photograph of her smiling straight at the camera. Like the friend she was there to support, she was young and beautiful.

Annie told the coroner she lived at 13 Holland Street, East Fremantle, which was not far from the Jacob house on High Street. Annie had met Audrey in Fremantle in June 1925, only weeks after Annie had arrived in the country from England in the March. Annie commuted to Perth for work during the week and after Audrey moved into Surrey Chambers, Annie started meeting her at the room. When asked about Audrey she said, 'She was my friend.' Arthur Haynes allowed the past tense of the statement to go without comment. Perhaps the police defence noted it.

Annie explained how she had convinced Audrey to go to the ball, despite her not wanting to, and had hoped that some social fun would cheer her up. They had been laughing on entry into Government House, and went on to have a good time on the dancefloor. Audrey caught sight of Cyril and this changed her mood. Despite her efforts,

Annie couldn't get Audrey to forget about her ex-fiancé, though there were moments of playful reprieve when they had supper with one of the male guests.

After midnight, Annie started to worry about the time. She needed to catch the 2.00 am charabanc back home to Fremantle. The friends agreed to leave after the thirteenth song but when Annie went looking for Audrey she couldn't find her. A short while later she saw Audrey, now out of her fancy dress costume and in a blue evening dress. A man asked Annie to dance with him so she was swept back onto the dancefloor. This was about 1.10 am.

The next time Annie saw her friend, Audrey was standing up at the balcony looking down at the dancers. Annie went up to her and said she needed to get her things from Audrey's room. Annie asked Audrey if she would come with her but she refused. Annie left and went to the cloakroom to get her coat. She saw Cyril Gidley again and went across to tell him that Audrey would like to speak to him. He said 'something to the effect' that he would.

Back at Audrey's room in Surrey Chambers, Annie took her wig off but covered up her fancy dress outfit with a coat. She changed, and left the building, walking back along St Georges Terrace to Government House. As she reached the grounds, an ambulance passed her. She hurried to the steps of the ballroom and heard what had happened.

'I saw Miss Jacob for a few moments in a small ante room near the orchestra in the custody of a policeman,' Annie testified. 'I still had the key to her room. She told me to keep the key and hand it to her mother.'

Later, while she was waiting for the charabanc to Fremantle, a police officer came up to Annie and asked her for the key. She handed it over to him.

Then came the question of a revolver. Annie hadn't seen one on Audrey all night and there was nowhere for her to have hidden it after she changed into her evening gown. But, as the police prosecutor noted, Annie had lost track of Audrey for some time, when it was claimed Audrey had gone back to her room to get the revolver.

It wasn't that Annie hadn't known about Audrey having a revolver. She was the one who had delivered it to her friend, courtesy of Jessie

5. 'SHE APPEARED TO BE IN A DAZED CONDITION'

Jacob in Fremantle. It was, she thought, about a week or a fortnight before the Government House ball that she had passed the revolver on to Audrey.

Strange things had been happening, which probably accounted for the revolver request. Audrey's diary went missing from her room in Surrey Chambers along with Annie's address book. Not long before Audrey moved to Perth, on 13 August, Annie went with her friend to Fremantle to visit Cyril Gidley on the *Kangaroo*. They met Cyril on the ship, he gave Annie a cup of tea and, in her words, 'we talked about England'. Cyril was interested to hear any news from back home and Annie had only been in Australia for a few weeks. According to Annie, they spent some time with Cyril and then she left at nine in the evening and Audrey remained. Annie saw Audrey the next day and she said she had 'made it up with Gidley'. He was going to call upon her or write. In Annie's words in court, Audrey 'appeared to be very fond of him'.

Arthur Haynes pressed Annie more about Audrey's feelings at the ball, allowing her to explain that what happened at Government House was embarrassing for Audrey. Cyril Gidley had 'publicly snubbed her'. Annie also thought there was more to this and that there had been another 'lovers' quarrel'.

William Vincent Murphy was called next. He had a very different story to tell. He worked as a Commonwealth civil servant at the Customs department and had known Cyril Gidley for about eighteen months. Cyril often visited him at his house on Carrington Street, Palmyra and it was there that William Murphy first met Audrey Jacob. The pair visited William and his wife, Violet, a number of times. William knew Audrey and Cyril were engaged and was given to believe it had been 'broken off'.

Cyril lived with the Murphys over October and November 1924 when he was on leave from his work on the *Kangaroo*. He was also living at their place when the search warrant was conducted for stolen goods but nothing was found.

Cyril later stayed at the Murphy house on 20 August and told William that he was not out on the *Kangaroo* because he had to undergo medical treatment by Dr Roy Mitchell, the father of Cyril's female friend, Maude. She was the woman who was dancing with him when he was shot.

William Murphy revealed that there had been a bit of an altercation on the *Kangaroo* on 11 August. Audrey had come to visit him on the boat. He told Audrey he was headed to the Mitchell's for dinner and escorted her off the ship. He walked her over the railway bridge and as they walked to the station Audrey said to Cyril that she would shoot him and then herself. This was a very different version to what Annie Humphreys had said about the visit. But Cyril appeared to take it as a joke, according to his friend, and he had told Audrey so.

William Murphy last saw Cyril alive at 12.15 pm on 26 August outside Michelides Factory on Roe Street, Perth. Outside the factory, Cyril told Murphy he wouldn't be home that evening as he was going to the ball at Government House. Murphy identified Cyril's body the next day in the morgue, along with Cyril's friend Edward Cutting, who organised the funeral.

Detective Sergeant Frazer went through Cyril's possessions on 30 August but missed one important item which William Murphy subsequently found. As Murphy explained: 'After Detective Frazer had gone I started to tidy the room and found on the bed an envelope now produced. The envelope was sealed up and only the word "She" written on it.'

Murphy opened the envelope and found a letter in Cyril Gidley's handwriting. He took it to the police the next morning. Marked as 'Exhibit L', the contents of the letter were presented to the inquest. The letter was read out:

> I, Cyril Gidley do hereby state that Audrey Jacob visited me on the above ship without my permission.
>
> While on board she tried to make herself a nuisance, and, rejecting her advances, threatened me with my life if I didn't make her my friend again.
>
> The reason I refuse was she turned me down, using her own words, 'I have got plenty of good friends on the

5. 'SHE APPEARED TO BE IN A DAZED CONDITION'

other ships.' This was just seven months ago, so I let her go to her good friends.
   (Signed) Cyril Gidley
   16.8.25
   PS. This note is in case she does keep her vow.

The newspaper reporters scribbled down notes as quickly as they could as this latest piece of scandal was revealed. William Murphy, Cyril Gidley's friend for the last eighteen months, was telling the coroner that Audrey had threatened to kill Cyril. This was damning evidence against Audrey when Arthur Haynes was trying to create a sympathetic picture of her against a negative portrayal of Cyril. The letter could also prove wilful murder over manslaughter. It would be hard to argue that Audrey had snapped for a moment upon seeing her ex-fiancé with another woman and decided to shoot him. If she had threatened his life days before the ball, it was premeditated.

Arthur Haynes was flabbergasted. He immediately called into question the legitimacy of the letter. How could it be that a thorough going-through of Cyril Gidley's belongings had been conducted and yet a letter of this importance was not found by the police? The press would include the letter in reports but rumours circulated that it was not Cyril's handwriting. The police were left to scramble and find out if it was his handwriting. They had been handed the evidence from Murphy and had taken it at face value.

Haynes also asked William Murphy if he had ever had an antagonistic attitude towards Audrey. Murphy replied that he hadn't and he knew nothing about the alleged schemes Cyril had created to keep Edward Jacob out of his home. He also knew nothing of Cyril spying on Audrey's father at a boarding house.

Violet Murphy took the stand next. She corroborated the main details of her husband's testimony and described Audrey's sapphire ring which she took to confirm her engagement to Cyril. She also saw Cyril on the day of the ball. He stopped by the house on his motorcycle at four thirty that afternoon and was all dressed for the ball. But first, he told Violet, he was off to have his picture taken at a photographer's studio in Fremantle. He had organised an appointment for 6 pm that evening and was keen to get there.

Cross-examined by Arthur Haynes, Violet Murphy confirmed Cyril had stayed at Spence's Boarding House and didn't much like that style of living. He said nothing to Violet of staying there under a false name, 'nor did he say anything about spying on anybody'. Further to this, avoiding the character assessment that Haynes was trying to create, Violet disagreed that Cyril was any kind of 'schemer or an actor'. Holding her ground, Violet told Arthur Haynes, 'As far as I am concerned he always behaved like a gentleman.'

The newspaper reporters would note that, at this point, Audrey leaned in and whispered something to her lawyer. Arthur Haynes then asked Violet Murphy if Cyril had 'kept company with her own daughter'. She said he had only taken her out on two or three occasions. Audrey seemed to know more than Mrs Murphy was letting on.

The inquest was adjourned to 10.30 am the next day, Tuesday 8 September. The first witness to be called by police was Russell Sandeman. He was a press reporter, residing at East Perth Hotel, and had been at the ball. He noticed Audrey enter the ballroom from the Wesley Wing and make her way to the centre, passing by other dancers.

'She had her eyes fixed on one particular couple and she passed between that couple and myself,' he told the coroner and court. According to Sandeman, Cyril had told Audrey he was 'engaged now' and would either see her later or after.

'Then what happened?' DS Frazer asked.

'I saw a movement of her right arm and at the same time heard a report.'

Cyril fell backwards, with his hands to his head. Sandeman hurried over to the vestibule and alerted Constable Wood, taking him to the dancefloor area.

DS Frazer asked Russell Sandeman if Audrey was excited.

'No', he stated, 'she appeared to me dumbfounded and not in the least excited.'

Arthur Haynes cross-examined Russell Sandeman and asked if he was 'quite close to the group', which he confirmed that he was. He

5. 'SHE APPEARED TO BE IN A DAZED CONDITION'

was also listening closely. Sandeman said he never heard Audrey say anything to Cyril Gidley: 'All the time I saw her she appeared to be in a dazed condition.'

Frederick Crowder, a resident of Adelaide Terrace, also gave evidence about what he saw on the dancefloor. Questioned by the prosecution, he said he had noticed Audrey and Annie earlier in the evening, notable in their fancy dress costumes. At about 1.25 am, he noticed that one of the women had changed out of her costume into a blue dress. He then saw her walking across the ballroom floor, in between dancers. The music stopped, Audrey walked towards a couple, and then the music started again. Frederick Crowder turned, lost sight of her for a moment, and then heard a shot. A man fell to the floor and Crowder rushed over to assist. He helped Sydney O'Neill carry the man to the cloakroom.

But it was Crowder's testimony about Audrey's words after the shooting which would cause a stir in the courtroom. Crowder claimed that as he knelt down at the injured man, he heard Audrey say: 'Well, I have got you now.' He looked up and saw the revolver in her right hand.

'Is the woman you saw holding the revolver here in court today?' DS Frazer asked.

'Yes,' Crowder answered, pointing over at Audrey.

Arthur Haynes was quick to cross-examine Frederick Crowder about Audrey's alleged statement.

'Was it you,' he asked, 'who started that canard about "I'll get you now"?'

'No, I distinctly heard it.'

Haynes queried whether it had been said in a whisper but the witness said it was in normal tone. Haynes pressed on: had there been anyone else between them when Audrey had spoken?

'No', Crowder replied, 'there was no one between us.'

Arthur Haynes was never going to be able to establish that Audrey had not shot Cyril. However, what he aimed to do was build a case around her altered psychological state, that she was not in her right mind when she shot Cyril. And it mattered if she had been clear enough to tell Cyril, 'I have got you now.'

Audrey's lawyer asked Frederick Crowder if he had read early reports about the shooting in the newspapers. He replied that he had but he knew that Haynes was trying to infer that he had lifted the words from the press and inserted them into his own testimony.

'I say,' he repeated to Haynes, 'she said it afterwards.'

Maude Mitchell was subdued as she entered the courtroom, still affected by the events of that evening weeks before. She had been dancing with Cyril Gidley when he was shot. By her own words, she had only known him 'a little' before the ball, but had fatefully had one dance with him, which would be his last. She recalled the last moments well.

The music had stopped and they were standing, waiting for the music to resume. Maude was looking at the orchestra and turned back to Cyril as the song started, and that's when Audrey came into view.

'I noticed a young lady standing a few feet away and I heard my partner say, "Pardon me I am dancing."' Maude took a deep breath. 'The next second he was shot …'

Unexpectedly, when asked about the woman who had shot Cyril, Maude looked out at the courtroom and responded, 'I am unable to recognise the girl in court.' Yet, she had been standing close to Maude when Cyril was shot and remained there for at least a couple of minutes while he was taken away to the cloakroom.

Cross-examined by Arthur Haynes, Maude confirmed she had met Cyril six weeks before when he called at her father's office. He said that his father had known Mr Mitchell back in England, that they had gone to the same school together. At the time, he did not mention Audrey Jacob or her family. Given than he was an Englishman, Maude's father invited him to their house and it was there, on the Sunday night before the ball, that he had been told about the event, and that Maude's mother was one of the organisers.

On further questioning from Haynes, she said she didn't think that she heard or that it was possible for Audrey to have said anything to Cyril before he was shot. She certainly hadn't noticed the young woman before that.

'After the shot was fired,' Haynes asked, 'did you see her stagger back a few paces?'

5. 'SHE APPEARED TO BE IN A DAZED CONDITION'

'No. I staggered myself, and was too upset to observe anything.'

Maude's father, Roy Mitchell, was called. He worked as a doctor in North Perth and had met Cyril two or three times, one of which was on 18 August 1925. He was unwell and Roy Mitchell advised Cyril to remain ashore and rest. Cyril consulted the doctor again on 24 August, two days before the ball, and was still receiving treatment. He had a cut on his skull, over his left ear, which he told Roy Mitchell was from a fall off his motorbike, trying to dodge a dog on the road. Cross-examined by Haynes, Mitchell revealed Cyril also had a scar on his abdomen which he said came from an altercation with a man on the *Kangaroo*. By itself, this was not important, but in terms of a character profile, Haynes was showing Cyril Gidley had been in a fight, perhaps reflecting a bad temper.

Detective Sergeant Joseph Frazer was also called to give evidence. He testified that Constable Wood had given him the revolver, which had five cartridges in the clip and one in the barrel. He also secured from Wood the empty cartridge that was now presented as evidence. In the hours that followed the shooting, DS Frazer went to Perth Hospital to collect Cyril's clothing, presented as 'Exhibit N', and which included his shirt, singlet, vest and dress coat.

'All the articles are perforated as if by a bullet on the left side,' DS Frazer told the coroner.

Frazer had searched Audrey's room at Surrey Chambers later on the morning following the shooting. He took possession of her fancy dress costume and found three revolver cartridges in a suitcase.

Cross-examined by Haynes, Frazer confirmed the safety catch was not on the revolver when it was handed to him.

Arthur Haynes called journalist and editor Victor Courtney to give evidence. His testimony would matter in terms of Audrey's mental state and anything she said at the time of the shooting.

Victor Courtney was in Government House around one thirty in the morning when he heard a shot. He rushed into the ballroom and it was then he saw 'a man just falling to the floor'.

'I went right to the scene,' he told Haynes, and watched Cyril being carried away. His attention then turned to the young woman who had shot him: 'I noticed every movement and action by her.' She was silent, and only spoke when the police arrived. She was dazed and 'did not appear conscious of what was going on around her'.

Courtney told the courtroom that he was a learned observer of events because of his newspaper work and so had watched Audrey closely with this in mind. Asked again about Audrey's actions straight after the shot was fired, Courtney confirmed he had not heard her say anything until the police arrived.

Police prosecutor DS Frazer cross-examined the *Mirror* editor, asking him: 'Did you hear her say anything?'

'Only when the constable approached. I heard her say something like, "Get me away from here quietly."'

Frederick Crowder's earlier statement that Audrey had said, 'Well, now I have got you,' was being brought into doubt by Haynes. Audrey's mental state was also being emphasised.

DS Joseph Frazer approached the bench and said he wanted to recall Victor Courtney to testify. He argued that Courtney could not have been as close as he said he was. From the vestibule he would have had to run thirty to thirty-five yards to reach the scene.

Coroner Kidson didn't allow for a recall, and the inquest was adjourned. Alfred Kidson needed some time to go back through the witness statements, sign his copies and consider their evidence. A courtroom appearance was one thing; the coroner needed to closely consider responses to questions and any doubt or falsities between evidence from witnesses to the shooting, and friends and family of the victim and the accused.

Audrey Jacob was taken back to Fremantle Prison. She watched the streets and familiar places pass by outside the police car and wondered what the coming weeks would bring. She had sat quietly through all of the evidence so far, taking it all in and trying to remember for herself all the details of that fateful evening. With a trial looming, Audrey would have to take the stand and defend her actions.

✦ ✦ ✦

5. 'SHE APPEARED TO BE IN A DAZED CONDITION'

The inquest resumed for its concluding day on Monday 14 September with Hubert Parker this time leading the police counsel. Allan Spence, a lumper who worked in Fremantle Port, was called. He said that his wife took in boarders at their place—known locally as Spence's Boarding House—and this was where Cyril Gidley came to stay the previous October. Edward Jacob was also staying there at the time and Cyril asked to be introduced as 'Douglas' to Jacob. He told Allan's daughter that he was there to spy on Mr Jacob who was doing his best to part Cyril from Audrey, who was now his fiancée.

Hubert Parker asked the witness: 'Gidley was always a decent fellow?'

Allan Spence replied that he was 'a bit of a swank'.

Parker continued asking Allan Spence about whether Cyril had gone looking for Audrey at her parents' house and hadn't found her, and her mother did not know where she was. But Allan knew nothing about this.

'Gidley told your wife that he had been to see Miss Jacob, but she was not at home,' Parker said.

Arthur Haynes interjected, unhappy with the tone of Parker's questioning: 'Who said so? Are you making a statement?' Parker replied that he was. Haynes objected to this, saying he had no right or capacity to do so: 'This is simple propaganda. They are trying to throw mud; the questions are loaded.'

Parker agreed: 'Exactly. There is a lot of loaded stuff in these.'

'Yes,' Haynes retorted.

Allan Spence then confirmed for Parker that he had never had any issues with Cyril Gidley and that, apart from being 'a bit of a swank', he had acted well around Allan's wife and daughter.

Arthur Haynes was now very keen to cross-examine Allan Spence. 'You can only tell us what you saw. You cannot say what happened behind your back?'

'No.'

'Did you come to my office voluntarily this morning?'

'Yes, on my own, and I could not stop my wife if she wanted to go. I tell you that.'

There was laughter at this in the courtroom. Coroner Kidson asked for quiet.

Haynes asked if Allan Spence had been asked to give a statement to the police and when he said he hadn't, Haynes replied, stingingly, 'We get only the leavings.' Clearly, he thought the police were not doing a very good job and perhaps withholding information from the defence.

The inquest fired up towards its end. Arthur Haynes expressed a concern about how the coronial inquest was being conducted. He claimed the proceedings were already being treated like a 'full-dress rehearsal for the criminal trial'. The coroner, he claimed, was too close to the police prosecution team. Coroner Kidson was a police magistrate, indeed, but he didn't take well to being accused of assisting the prosecution. The exchange between Arthur Haynes and Hubert Parker was a lively one, especially when Haynes also queried Detective Sergeant Frazer being an assistant to the coroner, making him a 'preparer of a case against the girl'. Arthur Haynes addressed the room:

> You can find that the deceased came to his death as the result of a bullet wound inflicted by this girl. Then you can commit her for trial on a charge of wilful murder, manslaughter, or whatever you think fit; but you cannot give a verdict as to anything except the cause of death. This is not a trial, and it is contrary to all the ethics of British justice that a person should be found guilty of an offence for which he has not been tried. As far as this Court is concerned, Audrey Jacob is not in custody and is not charged with any offence; and it is extraordinary that she should be found guilty of an offence with which she is not charged.

It was meant to be an inquest but Audrey, Haynes argued, was facing being judged as guilty by a coroner who should have just been determining the cause of Cyril Gidley's death. It was dramatic bluster from an experienced lawyer who knew Audrey would be going to trial

5. 'SHE APPEARED TO BE IN A DAZED CONDITION'

where he would have to cast doubt on police procedures, the treatment of Audrey on the night, and also monitor public perceptions of her. He was trying out his performance in the inquest first.

Audrey Jacob was not called to give evidence. Arthur Haynes told the coroner he thought it best for her, opting to protect her from the 'ordeal of the witness box'. Audrey listened on and knew what her counsel was doing. Protecting her from the witness box was one thing; Haynes was ensuring that she would not have to divulge sensitive material twice. It would be essential to do so in the trial to gain more sympathy for her when it really mattered.

There was more drama in the lower-court hearing when Haynes and Parker discussed Audrey's sister being called as a witness. Arthur Haynes argued that Cyril had been deceitful in his letters, stating that he could not find Audrey and when he went to her house, he had been told she was not there. Haynes also mentioned his frustration that he had not been allowed to call as many witnesses as those allowed for the Crown.

Hubert Parker objected to Audrey's sister being called (though she was not specified as either Enid, Verna or Vivienne), claiming it would not assist the coroner: 'If this child is allowed to give evidence, I am afraid I shall have to ask a lot of questions about domestic affairs.'

'That would be terrible!' Haynes sarcastically responded.

Hubert Parker was not impressed by his colleague's attitude. 'It would be terrible, and I don't want to do it.'

The coroner agreed with Parker and Audrey's sister was not called.

The inquest was concluded and Audrey Jacob was taken to a holding cell while the coroner retired to make his decision. It did not take him long, as he had known coming to the day's proceedings that there was really only one finding to be made.

Audrey Jacob was brought back to the lower court room from the holding cells and placed in the dock. She was asked to stand up by the court orderly. She stood quietly and nervously waiting for the coroner's decision. Suddenly Audrey was unsteady on her feet, shaking, and looking worriedly about her. Policewoman Helen Dugdale was there with her, as she had been for the last appearances. Coroner Kidson delivered his ruling:

> Upon inquiry I find that Cyril Gidley died at Perth on the 27th day of August 1925 from haemorrhage following a gunshot wound of the chest the result of a shot from an automatic pistol fired at the said Cyril Gidley by Audrey Campbell Jacob of Perth on the said the 27th day of August 1925.
>
> That the said Audrey Campbell Jacob did wilfully murder the said Cyril Gidley.

Audrey Jacob would stand trial at the next criminal sittings of the Supreme Court.

The courtroom waited for Audrey's reaction. Newspaper reporters waited, pens poised. She said nothing but looked straight ahead. Then Policewoman Dugdale took her from the room. Audrey would spend over three weeks back in Fremantle Prison waiting for the trial.

Later that day the *Mirror* would report: 'The first act in the greatest drama in the world, a trial for wilful murder, was over.' Well, it wasn't a trial and it wasn't over, and neither was it the 'greatest drama in the world', but it would continue to find its way into the national press.

DS Frazer left the courtroom knowing the task that was now ahead of him and other officers connected to the case. They would assemble all evidence to assist the prosecution case to ensure that Audrey would be found guilty of the wilful murder of Cyril Gidley. For the police, there was no grey area. Audrey had shot Cyril dead in the ballroom of Government House. There were various witnesses who saw Audrey walk across the dancefloor and shoot Cyril at close range. But DS Frazer knew what he and the prosecution were up against with Arthur Haynes. He would do his best to defend Audrey and cast doubt over the police case. Would a jury be swayed by this? Could Audrey Jacob hope to avoid a lifetime in jail or the hangman's noose? Executions were infrequent in Fremantle Prison and even more so when it came to women. The last—and only—woman to be hanged was Martha Rendell back in 1909 and now, over a decade later, it was no less shocking for a woman to be executed for a crime.

6. '... to blacken the character of the deceased'

Inspector Stephen Condon, Chief of the Criminal Investigation Branch in Perth, was given the Cyril Gidley murder brief and he knew what was needed on the ground. He put DS Joseph Frazer in charge of preparing the brief for the Crown Prosecutor. DS Joseph Frazer had close to twenty years as a constable and five years as a detective under his belt. He was close enough to those who could give a statement and they would not feel too much as if they were speaking to a superior. This would make them feel more comfortable about speaking freely.

Even before the Gidley murder, DS Frazer had worked some terrible cases. One of the worst was back in 1916 when he investigated the sickening sexual assault of an eight-year-old girl in a tent at the back of Claremont Drill Hall. The girl and her six-year-old brother had been passing by after leaving school when a returned soldier asked them to join him in his tent. He sent the girl's brother away with money to get some lollies and then assaulted the girl. The alarm was raised when the girl returned home and told her mother she had been in a tent with a soldier. The attacker was sentenced to two years imprisonment with hard labour. Like so many other police officers, Frazer was used to handling a range of crimes but it was always harder when the victim was a child.

DS Frazer would take nothing for granted in the Gidley murder case and it wasn't going to be as simple as proving Audrey Jacob's guilt. He went through the witness statements and his own notes, and summarised key details to report to the Crown Prosecutor. He could see what was already underway. Arthur Haynes was working to turn the attention back on the victim, and tell the story of how Audrey was worthy of sympathy after all that she had suffered at the hands of Cyril Gidley. So he ended the report to the Crown Prosecutor with a clear assessment of the state of affairs:

> All of the witnesses for the prosecution appear reliable. The witnesses for the defence appear to have been called simply to blacken the character of the deceased and contradict Crown witnesses whose evidence was against the girl (Audrey Campbell Jacob) in connection with the statements made by her after the shooting.

Inspector Condon read through Frazer's typed report and signed off on it on 15 September. It was then forwarded to the Commissioner of Police, Robert Connell. The Crown Prosecutor received the paperwork shortly after. On 21 September, a week after the inquest ended, Hubert Parker, as Crown Prosecutor in the case, wrote to Audrey's lawyer and asked if he would be 'raising the question of sanity of the accused'. If he was going to do this, Parker wrote, 'It will be necessary for us to have her examined by experts'. Parker needed a consent form for Audrey to undergo an examination. Parker was clear about why he needed this addressed: 'I do not desire to ask for an adjournment but to be ready to proceed on the 8th October next'. Arthur Haynes wrote back that he was not going to pursue the 'question of sanity' and now Hubert Parker knew what he was up against. Haynes was going to try for an acquittal.

Forty-one-year-old Hubert Stanley Wyborn Parker spent the next few days getting himself ready for the upcoming trial. The second child of eleven to judge Stephen and Ann Parker, Hubert was appointed to the position of Crown Prosecutor in December 1920. His brother, Frank, had also been the Crown Prosecutor but he was killed in World War One. Hubert too was a decorated war hero. He fought at Gallipoli and on the Western Front in France where he was

6. '... TO BLACKEN THE CHARACTER OF THE DECEASED'

wounded in September 1917 and awarded a Distinguished Service Order. He came back from the war and worked in the family law firm of Parker and Parker while also serving as president of the Returned Servicemen's Leagues before following in his brother Frank's footsteps into crown prosecution. Though he had at times considered going into private practice on his own, Hubert Parker enjoyed the challenges that crown cases brought for him. He knew the Cyril Gidley case in particular was an important one for both him and Arthur Haynes. And while he enjoyed a bit of sparring with Haynes on the last day of the inquest, Parker was intent on keeping Haynes restrained in the trial. He couldn't let the defence case gather the sympathy necessary to cast doubt over the wilfulness of Audrey's intent to shoot Cyril.

Hubert Parker was keen for the police to establish more background information about Audrey beyond that which had been revealed at the inquest. He knew there was more to her story than Haynes was letting on. And there it was in Frazer's brief. Edward and Jessie Jacob had visited Fremantle Police Station only months before the fatal shooting. They were worried about their daughter and her relationships.

Laura Chipper, signing off paperwork and statements as 'Woman Constable 1244', was asked to assist in the prosecution case against Audrey Jacob. On that last day of the inquest, Laura Chipper sat down at her desk at Fremantle Station and typed up a report detailing a meeting she had had with Edward and Jessie Jacob in May 1925, just months before the shooting at Government House. She hadn't thought too much of it at the time, given the number of parents making complaints about unruly children, but, as it would turn out, Audrey Jacob was not just another tearaway girl flouting social rules.

Jessie Jacob was alone when she approached Laura Chipper at the court house in Fremantle on 14 May 1925. She was nervous and concerned about who might see her there, knowing the gossip the rumour mill was quick to distribute around Fremantle. Jessie explained she wanted to see the policewoman about her eldest daughter who was 'giving a lot of trouble'. Audrey had been receiving letters from men on the ships docked at Fremantle port. It was all very awkward and embarrassing for her family. And Audrey's father was especially unhappy with her social life.

Policewoman Chipper took Jessie Jacob into a room and asked her to sit down. She wanted Mrs Jacob out of sight of anyone coming through the courts. Laura Chipper was well versed in being discreet. In her line of work, Chipper often uncovered the secret lives of young women in the city and their families wanted their secrets kept. Chipper was one of only a small number of women working in policing in the 1920s and their work was instrumental to protecting girls and women at risk.

Laura Chipper and her colleague Helen Dugdale were the first two women appointed as special constables in the newly created Women Police in 1917. Though policing had been around in Australia in one form or another since the colonies were established from the late eighteenth century, the work was only professionalised from the 1860s. It was another half century before women were considered for policing roles, firstly in New South Wales in 1915 and then the other states followed.

As the first two members of the Women Police, Chipper and Dugdale had an extensive work brief. Their duties were clearly about monitoring and policing their own sex. They were responsible for such things as keeping children off the streets, assisting the Education Department in preventing truancy, patrolling slum neighbourhoods, looking after drunken women, and keeping brothels, wine shops, and hotels under observation to protect girls and young women from being decoyed into prostitution. They had to keep a file for every girl and woman they assisted, detailing their movements and behaviour.

Laura Chipper and Helen Dugdale made their first public appearance when their position was announced to the Western Australian press in July 1917. Laura Chipper had been the matron of a Salvation Army rescue home and worked in social reform for fifteen years. Both she and Helen Dugdale were over the age restriction of thirty (Laura was thirty-eight and Helen was forty-one) but their experience was more important. Helen Dugdale was appointed based on her experience as a registered nurse and inspector in the State Children's Department. She was a tough Scotswoman who had married in Western Australia in 1912 but was now widowed. Both women were single and this was an important requirement of the job: their male superiors did not want women with ties, and especially women who had children to look after, who would distract them from getting the job done. As other female officers would reflect in the decades that followed, perhaps the greatest hurdle they faced was men who made decisions for women and reinforced the entrenched values of the time.

Chipper and Dugdale would each work under the Inspector of Police at the Metropolitan Branch and they would be directed to undertake the work given out to them. There were few opportunities for them to be a part of wider investigations, given their work was listed as a 'minor' branch. They were to wear plain clothes on the job, with the expectation this would create greater trust with women on the streets. Both women saw their work as providing important moral support around the city. Chipper and Dugdale, it was said, were keen to 'rescue' and reform women on the streets.

And they largely did the work with few other women to help. Female police numbers were limited in the first decades of operation. From 1917 to 1939, the Women Police consisted of, on average, around five females and never exceeded ten across the state. They were required to wear a hat and gloves and carry a handbag. This was all the protection they had.

In the early years of their work, Dugdale and Chipper kept detailed records of their interactions with women and children on the streets of Perth and Fremantle. In one annual report in 1921, Constable Dugdale had interviewed close to four hundred women in her office and cautioned a further 171 girls and women. Interviewing and meeting with women was another way in which they could exert their police authority and control women without having to resort to charges and imprisonment. They also met and were approached by the parents and families of at-risk young women and this was why Jessie Jacob had approached Laura Chipper.

Jessie held a letter in her hand from the commander of the sloop *Marguerite*. He was writing to ask Audrey to come to the ship about 3.00 pm that day. The commander, a Mr Langford, was married and this deeply concerned Jessie.

'I suppose that is where she is now,' Jessie said to Laura Chipper.

Jessie wanted Laura Chipper to give her advice about how to stop Audrey going on the ships and mail steamers and meeting men. Maybe there was something the Women Police could do to help?

Edward Jacob showed up at the office door and joined the meeting. He hadn't been far away, given he worked as a clerk of courts in the building, and through the meeting he would pop in and out. Edward said Audrey had been causing a lot of trouble in the family. In his words, she had been with a 'greaser' from the *Kangaroo* but they had 'got her off that now'. Except she kept visiting men on the ships, despite Edward pleading with the Company management not to let Audrey onboard ship. But still she was given passes and allowed onboard, coming back home with presents from the men.

'She wasn't getting them for nothing,' Edward told Chipper.

Audrey had been pushing the boundaries for a long while. She was smoking with friends and some of those friends also drank. They were worried Audrey was too. She was only twenty and yet seemed intent on keeping a questionable social life.

But things were far worse than this, according to Jessie Jacob. She pleaded with Laura Chipper that she didn't know what to do with her daughter. She was afraid of her—'she has a bad temper'—and would resent her parents visiting the police.

Edward was more scathing: 'I know she is no good, any girl who visits ships the way she does is no good and I want Mrs Jacob to realise it.'

There was also the matter of Audrey giving away her artworks to men on the ships, Jessie Jacob revealed. They were gifts to 'decorate their cabins, when she should have sold them to defray the cost of framing'. On one occasion, Audrey had come home 'with a sheet of stamps given to her by someone on board a ship'.

Jessie was embarrassed but told the policewoman: 'I found a French letter in her bag, and felt very worried about it.' It was scandalous

6. '... TO BLACKEN THE CHARACTER OF THE DECEASED'

that an unmarried young woman was keeping a 'French letter'—a condom—in her bag. Jessie lowered her eyes but Laura Chipper was not perturbed. Audrey was a young woman experimenting with being more independent and Laura had seen it in many cases. The worry, though, was always a pregnancy outside of marriage, knowing the stigma that came with this. There were homes where pregnant girls were sent and one of them was the Home of the Good Shepherd in West Leederville. In the confinement of doing laundry work and learning the ways of a good domestic life, these young women knew what it felt to be kept away from the prying eyes of society and not bringing disrepute to their families. But not Audrey Jacob. Her parents were intervening while they could.

Laura Chipper's report was forwarded to the Perth Criminal Investigation Branch (CIB) office, and was received by DS Frazer on 10 September. He included it in his brief for Hubert Parker. Frazer knew exactly how the information would be used. Hubert Parker would have at his disposal evidence that Audrey Jacob was no innocent art student led astray by an older man. And rather than being heartbroken and unable to get over Cyril, she had been seeing other men. It could also show that Audrey already had form for causing trouble.

The police also took a statement from a young pastoralist, Hermann Conrad Goerling. He had travelled to Perth early in July 1925 from Pinnacles Station but had family connections to Marloo Station, near Geraldton. The purpose of his visit was to see a dentist but he ended up crossing paths with Audrey Jacob. How the police came by this young man is not known. It could be that he approached police after knowing what unfolded at the ball and at the inquest, having read about it in the newspapers. What he offered was evidence the police could use to cast doubt over Audrey's lifestyle.

Hermann Goerling was staying at the Savoy Hotel in the city and had just finished dinner one evening when another hotel guest, a Mr Ramachioti, bumped into Hermann in the hotel lounge and told him about two ladies he was meeting. He pointed them out to Hermann 'sitting in the smoke room'. He couldn't say whether Mr Ramachioti had met the women before but when they walked out of the hotel and down the stairs, the women followed, where they stopped at the bottom of the stairs and another meeting was arranged for a few days later on Friday 17 July. Mr Ramachioti was interested in one of the young women's paintings which she was going to bring along to the next meeting.

They all met again on the Friday, outside the Piccadilly, around seven thirty in the evening. Mr Ramachioti had a flat up St Georges Terrace, near Milligan Street, and that was where they wandered to, in preparation for the display of the artworks. They had a small supper and glass of claret at the flat and left close to nine so that the women could catch the charabanc to Fremantle. Hermann now knew the young women as Audrey Jacob and Annie Humphreys. As he walked with Audrey, Hermann listened as she told him 'she had set her heart on being an artist and that she was going try and open a studio, but she was short of cash and her father would not give her anything'. There they left the women and the two men walked back along Hay Street.

This was not the last meeting. Hermann invited Audrey to the Savoy Hotel for dinner and, altogether, they met four or five times. They had dinner once during the week and on one Sunday evening. There was also a trip to the zoo. They talked more about Audrey continuing to pursue being an artist and Hermann recommended she study at the Technical School. He loaned Audrey some money towards her studies, which she was to pay back when she could afford it. They met one last time on Saturday 25 July—Hermann again loaning Audrey money—and they went to the Theatre Royal pictures, after which Hermann made sure Audrey was safe on the charabanc back to Fremantle.

Of itself, much of this was of little interest to the police, other than establishing that Audrey went into the city to meet young men and go on dates, but Hermann also spoke of Audrey's times aboard ships:

> When I used to meet her she told me that she used to meet the boats & go aboard the boats & have a dance or two, and that she knew a lot of captains & Engineers on several of the Boats and the afternoon when we were at the Zoo she showed me the miniature photo of an Engineer

6. '... TO BLACKEN THE CHARACTER OF THE DECEASED'

which she had in the back of her wristlet watch. She had two photos but I think they were of different men. Of the Engineer she said Sweet Memories or Memories of the past and I took it from what she said that she had finished with him.

Hermann was unable to say for sure that Audrey had mentioned the name of Cyril but when he read about the events at Government House the following month, he thought the name sounded familiar.

After Hermann went back to Marloo Station, he received another request for money from Audrey but he did not send any. The letter notified Hermann that Audrey was now living in Surrey Chambers in Perth.

What did the police have with Hermann's statement? Crown Prosecutor Parker could use it alongside Audrey's parents having raised concerns with Laura Chipper of the Women Police. It confirmed what the Jacob parents told her: that Audrey was meeting men on ships and she was trying to coax money out of Goerling to set up her studio. But was it really admissible in court when it would draw attention to the morality of the accused?

Cyril Gidley's shipmates on the *Kangaroo* arrived back in Fremantle Harbour on 26 September and were met by two detectives from the local Fremantle CIB branch. Their ship had left Fremantle back on 20 August, days before the fateful ball, and the detectives were very keen to talk to Cyril's workmates and friends to develop a clearer picture of him. The crew had only learned about Cyril's death when the ship berthed at Wyndham in the state's north on 15 September. Most people onboard were interviewed and the ship searched, including Cyril's cabin. The detectives talked at greater length with engineers on the ship and members of the engine room who had known Cyril better.

Truth newspaper got the scoop on the police visit onboard

the *Kangaroo*. According to reporters, Cyril was a popular officer and his mates spoke highly of him, taking issue with the character several witnesses had created at the inquest. He wasn't the least bit domineering, never had a bad word for anybody and one crew member even went so far as to say Cyril was 'probably the most popular officer on the North-West coast'. He was popular with the ladies, too, and though Audrey was one of them, the crew did not think she visited any more than anyone else. Cyril was, however, a bit of a 'ladies' man' and, as one of his closest friends recalled, 'like most seafaring men, he thought he had a girl in every port'. The crew were also surprised by the story that Cyril had been engaged to Audrey.

Yet, while the crew were supportive of Cyril, when asked why it had taken so long for the crew to find out about Cyril's death, the 'general opinion' seemed to be that, according to the newspaper, 'had it been known that Gidley had been murdered it was more than likely that his many friends onboard would have visited his cabin, and there would be the likelihood of perhaps certain things being 'dumped overboard'. But they were not given the opportunity and it is not known what the police did in fact find in Cyril's cabin.

So Cyril was a 'ladies' man' who liked the attentions of women. Audrey appeared to be one of a few women Cyril was interested in and his crewmates didn't believe he had made any commitments to her. Audrey had also spent time with other men and her parents were concerned about her visits to the ships to meet with captains. Audrey and Cyril appeared to be young people enjoying their independence and the attentions of the opposite sex. But, as the inquest had established, Audrey was caught off guard by seeing Cyril at the Government House ball and it completely changed the course of her evening, from an altered personality to a 'dazed' (her defence) or 'calculated' (the prosecution's) decision to shoot Cyril. The defence would be looking to 'blacken the character of the deceased', as DS Frazer believed, but the prosecution was also going to do its best in building up a case in which there was more to this innocent young art student than met the eye.

It was expected to be a memorable trial and it didn't disappoint.

7. 'It is a deliberate case of wilful murder': The trial begins

As the days passed by in her prison cell, Audrey had time to try to put everything together in her head. That moment back on the ballroom dancefloor seemed so long ago and yet was ever in her mind. What had she been thinking? How had it all come to this?

Her lawyer was certainly keen to know. He visited her at the prison and they went over her recollections of key events, aptly written on the back of pages taken out of the prison register. The thoughts and words flowed but it all seemed surreal.

'Our eyes met and he looked straight at me but never gave any sign of recognition.'

And how he teased her by talking to other girls: 'He then looked over in my direction with a smile on his face. I knew he was only doing this to hurt me.'

Arthur Haynes left, and she was alone again in this formidable place. Built by convicts and some free labourers in the 1850s, Fremantle Prison loomed over the port city from its vantage point on The Terrace, flanked on its southern side by Fothergill Street. Its limestone walls were also visible entering Fremantle from High Street and then turning along Hampton Road. The prison had been deliberately built in this spot so that it was far enough away from businesses in Fremantle centre but close to the police station and court house not far away on Henderson Street.

There in her grey-stone cell in the women's section in the north-western part of the prison, Audrey Jacob knew the seriousness of what she was facing. If found guilty of the wilful murder of Cyril Gidley, she could be executed by hanging on the prison grounds, not far from her cell.

'I felt a human being until the door of that cell at Fremantle gaol closed behind me for the first time,' Audrey would later say. 'After that I felt—well, just a creature, just a thing that the gaol would never let go.'

Audrey could see a little bit of sky through the window slit but struggled in the cramped conditions. She could reach out her arms from wall to wall. At night-time, she was scared by the dark and slept only in small 'fits and starts'. The rain would come in through the window and drip down on her face as she lay on the bed. During one cold evening, Audrey was convinced the ghost of Martha Rendell had come to her, readying her for execution. During the day, there were no terrors like those she suffered at night, but there was overwhelming loneliness.

Not far from where she was being held, Audrey's family were close to breaking point. It was hard enough that their eldest daughter was to stand trial for murder but the legal costs were stretching them too far. Jessie's brother in Essendon, Victoria was cabling details to Arthur Haynes of cheques he was sending to their brother in East Perth so that legal costs could be covered. At least £300 was mentioned in cables to the Haynes' family legal office in Perth.

The seams in the Jacob marriage were also once again strained. Jessie and Edward had to put on a brave, supportive front for their daughter in public but in private, there were still the same questions. What had Edward really been up to at Spence's Boarding House? When all of this was over, would their marriage survive? Should they have seen this coming? And would their daughter be condemned to death?

Thousands of miles away, Cyril Gidley's family in England waited for updates from family and friends. Newspaper clippings were being mailed over to them and Edward Cutting kept in regular contact. By

7. 'IT IS A DELIBERATE CASE OF WILFUL MURDER'

cable they learned that the coroner had ruled that Audrey Jacob had wilfully murdered Cyril and would now stand trial. Nothing would bring him back, but if justice was served, it might ease some of the pain of their loss.

✦ ✦ ✦

'Audrey Campbell Jacob,' the judge's associate addressed the accused, 'you stand charged by that name that on August twenty-seven, nineteen twenty-five at Perth, in WA, you wilfully murdered one Cyril Gidley. Are you guilty or not guilty?'

Audrey Jacob had unsteadily climbed the three steps leading up to the dock. She was dressed in the same cinnamon-coloured dress she had worn at the inquest but offset it with a dark sash. An overcoat hung over her arm and she held a hat of cinnamon colour to match her dress. She stood in the dock and answered, 'Not guilty,' before sitting down. Policewoman Helen Dugdale sat close behind her.

The Cyril Gidley murder trial was underway on 8 October 1925. People had been queueing outside the court since early in the morning, hoping for a chance to witness the drama. The public gallery was packed with spectators, notably a number of reporters jostling for prime viewing positions to hear evidence and note the reactions of witnesses.

Judge John Northmore addressed the twelve men of the jury as they 'kissed the book'—the New Testament—to seal their oath. He told them, 'You shall well and truly try and true deliverance make between our Sovereign Lord the King and the accused, and, a true verdict give according to the evidence.' He continued, 'The Crown has charged the accused with the wilful murder of Cyril Gidley. To this charge she says she is not guilty. It is your duty to hearken to the evidence and say if she is guilty or not guilty.'

Audrey trembled and policewoman Helen Dugdale checked that she was okay.

Looking at the twelve men who would decide Audrey's fate, Arthur Haynes wrote down in his case notes: 'First case I wish for female jury'. Both he and Hubert Parker had objected to some jury members: Haynes had objected to three and Parker to one jury member. Parker would later claim Haynes had deliberately supported Catholic jury members to suit his agenda in presenting particular information about Audrey.

Hubert Parker opened the case for the prosecution. The Gallipoli veteran, with his striking eyes, well-defined lips and deep voice, took to his feet and addressed the jury. The charge was a very serious one—wilful murder—but he wanted the members of the jury to dismiss anything they had read in the press: 'If you do, you will find your job much easier.' The Crown Prosecutor knew full well what Haynes was angling for with the press. Parker asked the men of the jury to focus on the evidence that would be presented in the courtroom. They would find that it 'is much different from what you have read'. He went even further, arguing that the decision must be based on what would be presented in the courtroom and 'not by what irresponsible people may have said or written'.

Parker had planned an opening statement that would not be lengthy but rather capture the main points of the prosecution case. He outlined the main course of events on that fateful evening in summarised form. They had been heard at the inquest but not before a jury. Audrey Jacob and Annie Humphreys entered Government House in their fancy dress costumes at eight thirty on 26 August 1925. About an hour after arriving, the pair saw the victim, Cyril Gidley, and noticed him on and off through the evening. Around one in the morning, as Annie and her male partner danced to the thirteenth song, Audrey told her friend she was going to the dressing room and they would meet after the dance. Annie failed to find her friend after the dance but she turned up after the next dance. She was now wearing a blue evening dress: 'they joked together about her having changed from a boy to a girl'. Audrey admitted she had been back to her room at Surrey Chambers to change and then left her friend, who soon after spotted her on the balcony overlooking the dancefloor. Annie went up to her friend and told her she needed to leave to collect her things from Audrey's room. This was about 1.25 am.

7. 'IT IS A DELIBERATE CASE OF WILFUL MURDER'

'Miss Humphreys,' Parker continued, 'asked accused if she was going home with her but accused said no, she would wait until Miss Humphrey returned.'

Annie Humphreys needed to catch the 2.00 am charabanc home to Fremantle and so 'had to keep an eye on the time'.

Audrey told her friend where to find the key to her room and 'as Miss Humphreys was leaving the accused, she asked her to tell the deceased that she wish to speak to him and tell him to come up to the balcony, and in reply to a question by Miss Humphreys stated that the deceased was in the lounge with a lady'.

Annie Humphreys left the ball.

Hubert Parker then focused his attention on the witnesses he would call. There would only be five of them, compared with eighteen called at the coronial inquest. On 25 September, Parker had written to the Commissioner of Police to inform him that he would not be calling Sergeant Brodie or Constable Timms as witnesses. Given how Arthur Haynes had criticised the actions of police in his cross-examinations at the inquest, Parker would not have wanted the same thing to happen to allow Haynes to guide the trial in a different direction, namely questioning the treatment of the accused after the shooting. Parker would also not be calling Audrey's parents, Allan Spence, Louis and Frank Cunningham, Fred Crowder, Roy Mitchell, Russell Sandeman, Victor Courtney or Matthew Waddell.

'Miss Mitchell will tell you that at about one thirty am she was dancing with the deceased,' Parker said. 'At the end of the dance just as orchestra started an encore, Miss Mitchell turned round to continue to dance when she noticed a young lady standing a few feet away and heard the deceased say, "Pardon me, I am dancing." The next second the young woman shot deceased and he fell.' Overcome by what had just happened, Maude Mitchell could remember nothing after that moment.

'Dr O'Neill will tell you that he heard a shot, turned round and saw a man lying about two yards away. He saw blood issuing from the mouth. He with others carried deceased out of the room. Blood and air was issuing from the nostrils. He died about a minute after being placed in the cloak room, having been unconscious all the time.'

'Dr MacKenzie will tell you that he conducted a post-mortem and found that deceased died from a gunshot wound in the chest and that he extracted a bullet; that deceased was shot just above the heart through the main blood vessel leading into the heart.

'Constable Wood will tell you that he was on duty in vestibule of the ballroom. He heard a shot and rushed in and saw a man on the floor. Someone said, "Look at the woman in blue." He saw the accused about six foot from the man and went over to her and caught her by the left arm, and at same time she said, "I did it." She had a revolver and he took it from her. The accused said, "Take me away."

'When Miss Humphreys returned she saw the accused for a few moments in a small anteroom near the orchestra in the custody of a policeman, and the accused told Miss Humphreys to keep the key of the room and hand it to her mother.'

Hubert Parker concluded his opening address by presenting a clear case to the jury: 'The facts are short, plain and simple, although it was a dreadful occurrence. This is a very serious case, gentlemen. It is a deliberate case of wilful murder.'

Crown witnesses were called. Annie Humphreys confirmed the main points the prosecution made about attending the ball with Audrey, seeing Cyril there and then her departure before the shot was fired.

Cross-examined by Arthur Haynes, Annie revealed it had been her idea to go to the ball and Audrey hadn't been interested. She had lain down for a couple of hours that morning, saying she did not feel well, and only decided to attend the ball after midday. Annie claimed Audrey had only danced with her, ignoring interest from male guests.

Judge Northmore asked Haynes if, in fact, men might not have danced with Audrey because she was in male attire? Haynes said he had 'often seen gentlemen dancing with ladies in male attire'.

The cross-examination continued and Annie offered more insight into her friendship with Audrey, saying that they had been at two other dances before the Government House ball; one was the police ball and the other was at the Piccadilly. At both, Audrey had been dressed as a lady and had refused to dance with any men, dancing exclusively with her friend.

7. 'IT IS A DELIBERATE CASE OF WILFUL MURDER'

Audrey had been shocked to see Cyril at the Government House ball, Annie told the courtroom. He was meant to have been away with work on the *Kangaroo*. Arthur Haynes then quizzed her about going to the ship on 13 August which Judge Northmore asked to be made more as a question of what she knew, rather than helping her by stating it. Annie claimed Audrey had written to Cyril and when they visited him on the ship, he claimed he had not received any letter.

'You could see she was very fond of him?' Arthur Haynes asked.

'Yes, she thought a great deal of him.'

'And from the way they acted that night?'

'Yes, they were quite friendly.'

As she had done at the inquest, Annie told of her address book going missing from Audrey's room at Surrey Chambers. Judge Northmore asked what point there was to this? Haynes said it would become clear and, turning back to Annie, he asked her about Audrey's missing diary as well.

'You know she was afraid because of someone hanging round her door previously while she was going to bed?' he asked.

'Yes.'

Audrey then asked her mother to send the revolver to her and it was received the next day. Annie had brought it to Perth with her, having collected it from Jessie Jacob.

Going back to the night of the ball, Haynes asked Annie about her friend's demeanour after seeing Cyril. She was now less lively, quieter, and despite Annie telling her to cheer up, she was changed by seeing him. Haynes pressed her on this, asking how Audrey seemed when Annie left to go to Surrey Chambers. She said Audrey looked 'weird' but when the judge queried this, she explained it as looking 'dazed and unnatural'.

The revolver was then produced as evidence. Annie confirmed she had seen it before: 'I did not see it closely in her room. That is the revolver so far as I can say.'

Hubert Parker re-examined the witness. He again raised their habit of dancing together at other balls and Annie confirmed this.

'Do you know if she refused any offers to dance with anybody?'

'I went to the cloakroom on several occasions and left her for a few minutes. As far as I know, no one offered to dance with her.'

'When Miss Jacob was living at Surrey Chambers was she in employment, or was her time her own?'

'Her time was her own.'

'Was she in an occupation which would prevent her from going to Fremantle if she had wished to do so?'

'No.'

'You spoke of a snub at the ball. Was it such that would have been noticed?'

'People who knew both of them would notice it.'

'It was not so much what he did as the way he did it?'

'Yes, that's what I mean.'

Arthur Haynes was quick to follow up on Parker's attempts to show Audrey was living a carefree life, going to balls with her friend, and not working.

'As you know accused came to Perth to follow up her painting at which she was rather proficient. As there was no opening to study at the moment, didn't she do some paintings in her rooms?'

'She had done a couple of paintings,' Annie answered. 'For the two days before the tragedy she had been attending painting classes. I saw the paintings she had done.'

Maude Mitchell's testimony was the same as she had given at the coronial inquest. She told the prosecutor she had not danced with Cyril before the fateful one in the early hours of 27 August. Maude hadn't noticed Annie and Audrey in fancy dress costumes but as she danced with Cyril, she noticed a young woman approach. She was a few feet away and all Maude heard was her dancing partner say to the woman, 'Pardon me, I am dancing.' She couldn't remember hearing the shot but recalled Cyril falling to the ground. She also did not see Cyril publicly snub Audrey.

Cross-examined by Arthur Haynes, Maude revealed she had met Cyril three times before, one of which was a Sunday dinner. Cyril had not told her about Audrey, her family, or their engagement. Pressed by the defence, she testified she had not heard Audrey say anything to Cyril before he was shot.

Doctors Sydney O'Neill and Donald MacKenzie were called for the

7. 'IT IS A DELIBERATE CASE OF WILFUL MURDER'

prosecution. Though they were there to give evidence about the post-mortem and Cyril's condition, Haynes used his cross-examination as an opportunity to cast doubt over exactly where Audrey had been standing. If she had been a few feet away, as some witnesses and the police argued, the bullet could have gone straight through Cyril's body? Dr MacKenzie could not confirm this definitely but it could have been possible.

Why did it matter where Audrey had been standing? Because, as Arthur Haynes was going to establish, taking a few steps back meant that Audrey had positioned herself to shoot Cyril. And that is not what he was going to argue about his client's actions at the ball.

Constable John Wood was called next. He repeated what he had said at the inquest, that he heard a shot, ran from the vestibule and saw a man lying on the ground. Someone nearby said 'Look to the woman in blue' and that was when he saw the accused standing about six feet from the victim. As he approached the woman, she said 'I did it' and was holding a revolver in her right hand. He took the gun and found that it was loaded and cocked. The woman said 'Take me away' and so he did.

Arthur Haynes cross-examined the constable, asking: 'The pressure on the trigger is likely to fire the revolver more than once?'

'Not in my experience,' he answered. 'The trigger has to be pulled again.'

Then there was a bizarre altercation between the two lawyers after midday in which Hubert Parker made the claim he did not think Arthur Haynes would admit the body was that of the deceased.

'I have said before I can admit nothing,' Haynes responded.

'In that case,' Parker told the judge, 'I will close my evidence, except that I will call someone from the morgue to identify the body.'

The trial was adjourned to two that afternoon.

Customs officer William Murphy was called for the prosecution after the break. He had known Cyril Gidley for eighteen months and was the one who had identified his body at the morgue. Yes, it was him, there was no doubt about that.

Arthur Haynes cross-examined William Murphy and asked about Cyril's relationship with Audrey. Murphy had known they were engaged and she visited Cyril sometimes at the Murphy house, when Cyril was staying there. Murphy knew Cyril was also at the boarding house but he knew nothing about him staying there under an assumed name.

Parker re-examined the witness. 'You knew Gidley and the accused were engaged?'

'Yes, and that the engagement was broken off.'

'How did you know he was engaged?'

'He told me, and I saw the announcement in the papers.'

'How long after the engagement was announced did you know the engagement was broken off?'

'About four months after; after October, that is.'

'Was that announced in the paper?' Arthur Haynes now asked.

'No, it was what I was told.'

Justice Northmore queried what Haynes was trying to establish: 'Is that any better or worse because it was announced in the paper?'

'One is entitled to give it credence when it appears in the paper.'

It was a casual nod to what he thought about the newspaper business and his friends in it.

8. '... things are not always what they may seem': The trial continues

The prosecution case having now been stated, with the opening address and witnesses, Hubert Parker took to his seat in readiness for the start of the defence's case. Parker was confident of the main details he had laid out and the evidence developed from the witnesses and the various exhibits. But now, as Arthur Haynes stood to open his case for the defence, Parker watched his sparring partner closely—a man he had seen build up an impressive brief over the last few years.

It was Arthur Haynes' turn to grab hold of the jury's attention and turn them in favour of his client: 'The Crown, through its representative, will put it to you that this is a very simple case with a very simple issue, and, of course, with a great degree of self-complacence, he will assume that you will have no difficulty in coming to the conclusion that this girl wilfully murdered the deceased man.

'Gentlemen, you should remember that things are not always what they may seem on the surface, and you will find that that applies to this case. I hope, as my friend put it to you at the outset, that you will keep an open mind on this subject, and not allow outside circumstances, rumours, and so forth, to influence you.

'Certain things have been published, and, we know, have reached the knowledge of practically every person in the community. There were things heard at the inquest that you will not hear of here.

Furthermore, all sorts of bogus rumours have been circulated, as happens in every sensational case, and one of these has reached me from several sources, and which you might also have heard, was that the Crown reduced the number of witnesses it had at its disposal because of some sort of arrangement that the accused would plead guilty.'

Haynes paused and let this statement sink in for the jury. 'I do not know if that reached you, but, if it did, I say chuck it out of your mind. Nothing could be more absurd. I want to appeal at this stage for fair play to this young girl, who is charged with the most serious offence the law knows. I want the opportunity to place the whole facts before you, to develop the defence properly and give the whole of the circumstances surrounding the accused, so that you will be able to intelligently understand the position in which she is placed. I want you to see the whole picture. I think the circumstances I will reveal to you will justify, if not demand, a verdict of not guilty from your hands.'

Audrey sat quietly in the dock, watching her lawyer. She was confident Arthur Haynes would represent her because he had reassured her he could set up the case to swing in her favour. This meant turning the shooting victim, Cyril, into an unlikeable character who had pushed Audrey to her limits. And he would also look for sympathy for his client:

'She has been under arrest since August twenty-six last—about six or seven weeks. During that time she has been shut up in prison. She has never been in court before in her life, that is, prior to the previous Police Court proceedings. Even although she may not appear to you to be shaken violently before you, you must remember there are deep-seated emotions which are not visible on the surface. The story as I shall unfold it to you will justify and I think even demand a verdict of "Not guilty".'

Audrey's lawyer then set out a consideration of 'the parties in this affair'. Audrey Jacob was twenty years of age. She was from a large family of eight children and her parents lived in Fremantle, where her father was a clerk of courts. She had been educated at the Roman Catholic Convent in Norseman when her father had worked as a clerk of courts in the town.

Hubert Parker noted this point down. There was no evidence that Audrey had in fact been educated in a convent, but perhaps the officers putting his brief together had missed this? What he didn't know at the time, and which he would later fume over, is Audrey had only converted to the Catholic faith days before the trial. And the speed of this process was questionable, given the time it ordinarily took to take up the faith.

It was in the convent, Haynes continued, that Audrey developed a 'talent for painting'. She had been painting for the last three years, after leaving school, and had sold many of her works, 'mostly to officers of boats, who have distributed them all over Australia, and practically the world, by now.'

On this point, and perhaps knowing about Audrey's parents approaching the police about her visits to the ships, Haynes said Audrey had a cousin who was a wireless operator working on one of the mailboats. It was from this connection that Audrey had met officers interested in buying her artworks. Audrey met Cyril on one of the ships and they started a lengthy association over the course of two and a half years but Cyril Gidley was of questionable character:

'Gidley told accused and her parents that he had been sent from home on a five years probation, and if he conducted himself properly he would be received back home, and if he married a girl like accused he would restore himself to his proper place with his own family.'

And then came the main point of the defence case.

'I do not like to speak harshly about people who have departed, but the facts have to be spoken. It would be shown that deceased was a cool, calculating schemer from the inception.'

Haynes' long opening statement made it very clear what the members of the jury would be taking into account as evidence for the defence. Cyril Gidley was a smuggler. He smuggled goods into the country and coaxed a friend into storing the goods for him. Cyril avoided Audrey's father, for fear of being caught out in his smuggling efforts, and worked to alienate him from his family. He and Audrey became engaged in September or October of 1924 and Cyril continued what Haynes called 'his insidious propaganda' against Edward Jacob. He came across as genuine in his concerns about Edward's unfaithfulness to his wife and it was in this way that he was able to reel Audrey and her mother into believing him:

'One can imagine,' Haynes said, 'the mother's feelings with the cares of a large family and the trouble attendant upon it, and the two highly strung people. The resultant quarrels were the fruits thereof. It culminated in August, nineteen twenty-four, in the father leaving her and the mother issuing a summons through a solicitor against her husband claiming separation and maintenance. She set out the ground of separation as cruelty. There was no cruelty such as would warrant any order being made but, of course, some ground had to be submitted.'

With Edward Jacob absent from the house, Haynes explained to the listening jury, Cyril tried to take control and coax Jessie into adding two extra rooms to the house to store his smuggled goods. Jessie refused and shortly after, Edward bumped into Cyril in the street and angrily asked him what his game was in trying to separate him from his wife? Cyril goaded him, saying he knew a lot of things, and then revealed that he was going to marry Audrey, to which Edward clearly objected.

Haynes revealed further stories about Cyril having been friendly with a woman in Bunbury and she had gotten it into her head they were engaged. He had given her a ring but he got it back through trickery, according to Arthur Haynes. There was another woman, back in England, who also believed they were engaged and she wanted to join him in Australia. All of this would later play on Audrey's mind, especially the rumour that Cyril had a 'stock of engagement rings'. Haynes continued:

'When he became engaged to her, he produced three rings. He said he bought three different sizes to see which would fit. He put one on her hand to see whether it would fit. Sometime afterwards he said he would slip one on her hand, and it was such a tight fit it had to be filed through the following day. As I said, he carried a stock of them.'

The Cyril Gidley that Arthur Haynes was detailing for the jury was cruel and manipulative. He taunted Audrey about letters she still received from a former boyfriend and on one particular evening, when he had lured her to the Murphys' house, making her think the Murphys would be there and they were not. They got into an argument, reducing Audrey to tears. Cyril had picked her up, against her will, and taken her to his bedroom, where he put her down on the bed: 'She struggled with him, but her struggles were of no avail, and, to put it shortly, he seduced her against her will.'

Now the defence case took a remarkable turn. As the paper reported:

> You may ask, did she cry out? She did not. She fought against him but was overpowered. After that he said he would go and see Mrs Murphy, and ordered her to the bedroom to do her hair. She did so, and Gidley shortly afterwards returned with Mrs Murphy. Accused met them on the back porch, where she could not be clearly seen. During the struggle, he caught her by the throat, and shoulder, and when she reached home she could see marks there.

Evidence would be presented to support this version of events, and the word 'seduction' would be used in place of sexual assault or rape. Audrey's mother had seen her that evening and she had seen the marks on her body. Cyril had walked Audrey home that evening and pleaded with her not to tell her mother. But Jessie Jacob knew something was wrong with her daughter. She would usually come into her mother's room for a brief chat before going to bed. She had gone straight to her own room. Jessie was worried and enquired in on her daughter who said she was fine but was trying to cover some bruises. Jessie Jacob, Haynes explained, also found evidence when doing the washing the next morning which clearly indicated what had happened to her daughter.

Audrey broke down at this point. Her sobbing could be clearly heard and Haynes paused to make sure she was being comforted by the policewoman with her.

The building of a cunning profile for Cyril continued, with him forcing Audrey to take on an assumed name and move to Perth. Then he left letters at her family home in which he claimed he had come to call on her and did not know where she was. He said she had been a good daughter but had been ill-treated at home and the return of her father was a problem. But though Audrey felt under duress in following Cyril's commands, she went to see her mother shortly after and told her the letters were false. Cyril saw Audrey soon after, on a tram in Fremantle, and gave her bogus stories about needing the engagement ring back. He later threw it into the sea, making it clear the engagement was over.

Things deteriorated further when Edward Jacob confronted Cyril about smuggling goods and his relationship with Audrey. Cyril threatened to kill Edward and Audrey's father was so shaken by the threat that he made a complaint to Detective Sergeant Cowie at Fremantle Police Station. But, despite, everything she and her family were going through, Audrey was in love with Cyril:

> During this time the accused was very much in love with the deceased. She could see no fault in him. It always happens that when a girl is deeply in love with a man she only sees his good points, and smooths the bad ones over. After all, she is only a girl.

Audrey had composed herself in the dock by now but she would break down again during the course of the trial, not least when she had to take the stand and confirm what her lawyer was setting out in her defence.

Arthur Haynes set out the defence version of events from the evening of the ball, which he would then draw out again when Audrey took the stand. But it was the mental state of his client that he chose to emphasise here and then reiterate via Audrey's testimony. She was 'quite unconsciously' carrying the revolver, wrapped in a silk handkerchief. She neared Cyril and placed her left hand on his shoulder. He dismissed her by saying he was dancing. She was in a daze. It was the final insult. She threw her hands to her forehead and that was all she remembered.

Haynes claimed that Audrey did not properly regain her composure until hours later in the cell at the lock-up. She had been in a daze, didn't see Cyril fall, nor hear the report from the gun. And then, coming out of this state, she found herself in a cell being questioned by police officers.

8. '... THINGS ARE NOT ALWAYS WHAT THEY MAY SEEM'

It took a lot for Hubert Parker not to react to this. He knew that Detective Sergeant Frazer had visited Audrey by himself and he hadn't taken the moment lightly. She was a young woman who had committed a terrible crime but was still deserving of care in the lock-up. But this would be lost because Haynes was putting on a good show in his defence of Audrey.

Arthur Haynes closed his opening speech by looking directly at Audrey and connecting with her to gain more of the sympathy of the jury. It was three thirty in the afternoon and all the courtroom waited for Audrey to take the stand.

Audrey Jacob left the dock slowly. She and Haynes had gone over the key details she had set out for him and she had practised her responses to his questions. She took the oath in a quiet voice but was asked to speak up, which then meant she nervously spoke faster and the stenographers had to catch up:

> I was born in Western Australia and I am 20 years old. My father is clerk of courts at Fremantle. I have seven brothers and sisters. Until recently I lived with my parents. I was educated at a Roman Catholic Convent at Norseman until I was 16. Among other things, I learnt painting, then a little over three years ago my father was transferred to Fremantle, and we have lived there ever since. I have kept up my painting, and have sold 200 to 300 of my works.
>
> Through a cousin who is on a mailboat I met a Mr Claude Arundel, who is a ship's officer, and after a short acquaintance became engaged to him in July, 1924. I had known Cyril Gidley for over two years. I used to meet him when his boat was in port and sometimes went to the pictures with him.
>
> In August, 1924, the *Kangaroo* was in port. Gidley was 6th engineer on the boat. When on shore that time Gidley asked me to break my engagement with Mr. Arundel and become engaged to him. I asked for time to consider it. The *Kangaroo* went to Singapore, and when she returned Gidley again pressed his suit. When I realised he was

serious I consented to marry him, and our engagement was announced early in October. He had six weeks leave then, and owing to a strike was on shore for about four months altogether.

Arthur Haynes now needed to go into detail about Audrey's home situation but Hubert Parker objected that it was not relevant. Haynes pleaded with Judge Northmore, that it was:

> My task is very difficult, Your Honor. This is a case in which the human emotions play a great part. And I want, all the surrounding circumstances to go to the jury so that they may judge what was passing through this girl's mind. I submit that the happenings in the home through Gidley's influence had a great effect.

Judge Northmore admitted, however, that while he didn't think the home situation had nothing to do with the shooting, he was sceptical about whether it had anything to 'with the answer'. He didn't want the case degenerating into accusations and hearsay. Haynes acquiesced and then asked Audrey about an estrangement between Audrey's parents because of what Cyril Gidley had said.

Judge Northmore interjected: 'Now, Mr Haynes, that is not relevant.'

'I only want a fair go,' Arthur Haynes replied.

'Quite so, but …'

Haynes directed his attention back to Audrey. 'Did your father leave home, anyway?'

'Yes.'

'Did your father stay at Spence's boarding house?'

'Yes, and Gidley said he would stay there also under the name of George Douglas to keep an eye, on him.'

'I want to keep the case to what is relevant,' Judge Northmore directed Haynes.

'Of course the revolver didn't go off then. If we're to start weeding out …'

'Well, I rule that matter out, anyway.'

Haynes turned back to Audrey. 'During the four months Gidley was on shore, how often did you see him?'

'Almost every day.' And then Audrey detailed how, after a while, Cyril went to stay at Murphy's place and it was there he hurt himself with an axe. Audrey visited him after noon each day.

Haynes asked his client about Cyril's cruel side:

> It was November 8, I think. We were starting off for Murphy's place when mother gave me a letter from Mr. Arundel. I put it in my bag, and on my way I asked Cyril if he objected to me reading it. He said 'No' so I opened and read the letter, Cyril said Mrs. Murphy had invited us to spend the evening with her as her husband was on night duty. When we got there we went into the kitchen and Cyril switched on the electric light. It was about half-past six when we left home to go to the Murphy's. I naturally asked where Mrs. Murphy was, and Cyril said she had gone to Mrs. McGregor's place. I then asked him why he had deceived me.

'What did he say to that?' Haynes asked

'You wouldn't have come with me if you knew we'd be alone.'

Audrey then spoke about their arguing over the letter she had received from her former fiancé. Cyril had shown no objection to her reading it but then, suddenly, was defensive and asking her how much she still thought about Claude Arundel. Then he started being kind to her once more and things escalated from there:

> I was still crying. He picked me up in his arms and carried me into his bedroom. He put me on the bed. He had his arms around me and said to me several times: 'Say yes.' I knew by his actions what he meant.

In the witness stand, Audrey muttered something inaudible, bent her head and started sobbing. She stopped a short moment later but when she lifted her head to continue on, she couldn't. She drank back some water. Judge Northmore asked if she had said 'yes'.

'No.'

Arthur Haynes continued: 'Did he do anything, Miss Jacob? Did he overpower you in the bedroom or not?

'Yes, he did.'

'Afterwards he went for Mrs Murphy?'

'Yes.'

''On the way home did he ask you to refrain from doing anything?'

'He asked me to promise not to tell my mother.'

'Did you promise?'

'After a while I did. That was while we were walking home. I went straight into my room. Mother called to me, because I always used to have a little chat with her when I came in. She came into my bedroom. I was crying. She noticed marks on my throat and asked what had happened, and I said I had bruised myself. Next day Cyril called, and mother refused to see him. I told him, "She has guessed everything. She saw the marks on my throat."'

Audrey found it hard to continue but managed to explain that her father was then due to come home. Cyril told her she had to move out and so arranged for a room to be held for her in Perth under an assumed name. Audrey explained how their relationship suffered from his cruelty and trying to take her away from her parents. Their engagement was over, with the dramatic story told of the ring being thrown into the ocean, and Audrey left home again to live in Surrey Chambers while she took art classes. She remained on good terms with Cyril, however, and visited him on the *Kangaroo* for several hours during one visit and more briefly for another. She became concerned once more, however, when her diary and some letters went missing from her room.

'Now we come to the day of August twenty six, the Wednesday,' her lawyer continued. 'Who asked you to go to the ball?'

Audrey explained that it had been her friend, Annie Humphreys, and that despite her being unwell that morning, with a terrible headache, she was eventually persuaded to go.

'We arrived at the ballroom about eight thirty pm. I danced with

8. '... THINGS ARE NOT ALWAYS WHAT THEY MAY SEEM'

Miss Humphreys all the evening. One or two gentlemen asked me to dance with them, but I refused. At about nine o'clock I saw Cyril Gidley near the door. As we passed, his eyes and mine met, but he didn't recognise me.'

Judge Northmore asked Audrey: 'Was that the first time you saw him at the dance?'

'Yes.'

'Did you see him again?'

'Yes, I saw him frequently as I continued to dance with Miss Humphreys but he refused to recognise me. He passed me four or five times—more, in fact—but he was very cold.'

Audrey now set out the public humiliation she had suffered: 'Sometimes he would, look at me and put his chin up. Several times as he passed me he gave a bit of a sneer and then turned away and laughed. He was talking to a young lady in a heliotrope dress and laughing. She turned to run up the stairs, and he ran after her and pulled her down. Then he looked up at me. I knew he only did it to annoy me.'

'What sort of a man was he?' Haynes asked his client.

'He was rather a domineering person. It's very hard to explain. He was the living embodiment of the Sheik.'

'And what was your feeling towards him?'

'I was very fond of him.'

And back to that fateful evening:

'I was feeling very upset and ill and my head was aching. I went to my room and lay down on the bed and cried for about half an hour, I think, then I started to undress. When I opened a drawer I saw the revolver, and then I decided to end my life. So I started to dress again. I meant to go down to the foreshore to end my life. I didn't put on the Pierrot costume, because I didn't want to do it in a fancy dress. I picked up the first dress handy, which happened to be a blue costume hanging over the end of the bed.'

'That was an evening dress?'

'No, it wasn't an evening dress. It was a costume suitable for the afternoon or evening. I wrapped the revolver in a handkerchief and went out intending to go down to the foreshore. But on the Terrace I changed my mind and decided to go to the Catholic Cathedral first and say my rosary. I wanted to make my peace with God. I went inside the gates of the Cathedral where I knelt down. I had my beads and I said my rosary.'

Audrey now explained how, though she felt better, her head was 'queer' and her 'heart was aching'. She decided against taking her life and 'determined to go home'. As she did, she passed Government House and went into the ballroom where she could see people still dancing, including Cyril.

'I went in, but I couldn't see him at first. I saw Miss Humphreys and asked her to send Cyril to me on the balcony. After a time he came, and stood under where I was and looked up at me, then turned away with a nasty look. I felt that I must know what was causing him to treat me like this.'

The dance stopped and Audrey went down to the floor and stepped forward to where Cyril was. The music started again, and Cyril hurried back to his partner. Audrey followed him and touched him on the shoulder with her left hand. In her recollection, Cyril had told her he was dancing and said it in a 'haughty manner'.

Now came the fatal moment.

'Then something seemed to snap in my head. I don't remember any more. Everything seemed to be going round and round. When I came to my senses I was in a cell in the lock-up.'

'Did you have any intention of causing Cyril Gidley any injury?'

'No, none whatever.'

'Ever threaten or wish him any harm?'

'No. If I could I would undo what has been done.'

It was now after five in the evening. Hubert Parker stood up, ready to cross-examine the accused. He asked Audrey about her visits to boats in the port. Arthur Haynes intervened and so began a discussion between the two about evidence and reflecting on the character of the accused.

'I have no intention of making any reflection of her character,' Parker replied.

The judge agreed: 'Then don't make any reflection. So far there is nothing against this girl's character.'

Audrey told the courtroom that her mother always waited up for her and knew of her meetings with Cyril.

'And she never objected?' Parker asked.

'No.'

'Didn't she make a complaint once about another man?' Parker was referring to Jessie's visit to seek the help of policewoman Laura Chipper.

'No, never.'

'But,' Parker continued, 'she complained once about something she found in your bag?'

Audrey responded indignantly: 'That had nothing to do with this affair at all. And she did not make a complaint.'

Arthur Haynes interjected and claimed that Parker could not refute the story and so was 'throwing stones'.

'I did not say I could not refute the story,' Parker replied, 'and at all events I'm not throwing stones at someone who is dead.' It was a poignant dig at the defence lawyer and his case against Cyril.

Hubert Parker directed his attention back to the accused: 'Are you surprised to know that no rings were found among Gidley's belongings after his death?'

'He may have given them away to other women.'

'What earthly use would your diary, which you say was stolen, be to Gidley?'

'I don't know?'

'Did it have anything in it that you would not have liked Gidley to see?'

'No. Anybody would have been at liberty to read it.'

The prosecutor asked Audrey more about her relationship with Cyril and whether she had been respectable with him. They would often meet at the gate of her parents' garden, where they would talk for a long time. Gidley only 'seduced' her once.

Arthur Haynes objected again to the questions and while Hubert

Parker said he had no intention of making suggestions about the 'girl's character', the judge told him not to do so and that it was irrelevant anyway. The details of Laura Chipper's statement about the 'french letter' would now not be detailed.

Judge Northmore, noting it was past six o'clock, adjourned, telling the courtroom the trial would resume the next day.

Spectators hurried out of the courtroom, making what they wanted to out of the opening addresses and Audrey's testimony. It was hard not to feel for the young woman. If what she was saying was true, Cyril Gidley had terrorised her family and she had just publicly told of being sexually assaulted by him. It didn't mean she had the right to take justice into her own hands, but it might explain why, seeing him with another woman and publicly slighting her, she had gone into some daze and resolved to make him notice her.

Had she really forgotten the revolver in her hand and been as surprised as everyone else when it went off?

Hubert Parker had a lot to think about that night. He had started the trial with what he thought was a strong case. It was clear Audrey Jacob had shot Cyril Gidley. There were witnesses who placed Audrey on the dancefloor shooting Cyril. Police officers had testified that she admitted her guilt. Parker thought this was a clear wilful murder case but Arthur Haynes was taking it in another direction. Audrey claimed Cyril had been abusive and cruel. But this was not grounds for finding her not guilty. Hubert Parker knew Haynes was pushing an accidental shooting case. Parker was not convinced of this and neither were the police officers there at the ball that evening and others who helped to put together his prosecution brief. But it mattered little what the police believed. Parker had to convince the jury that Audrey had intended to shoot Cyril and that *he* was the real victim.

9. 'In The Shadow of the Gallows': The verdict

The second day of the trial continued as dramatically as it had started. Crown Prosecutor Hubert Parker continued his cross-examination of Audrey and questioned her about her friendships with other men. Audrey claimed Cyril knew about her friendships with other men, and he was fine with it, so long as they were respectable. Parker wasn't convinced but he didn't push it any further, taking note from the day before that maligning Audrey's character would be frowned upon by the judge.

He came back to the night of the ball. Parker asked Audrey about her actions before going back to Government House and shooting Cyril. Especially her decision to take her own life.

'If you were going out to shoot yourself, why did you bother about hiding the key at all?'

'I hid it simply from habit.'

'You had made up your mind to shoot yourself beside the river, and yet, instead of at once walking towards the river, you went up Howard Street, and along St Georges Terrace. Why was that?'

'It was not until I was walking along the terrace that I decided to end my life beside the river.'

'When you left your room you did not know where you would do it?'

'No.'

'You say that when you decided to go to the Roman Catholic Cathedral you had your rosary beads with you. Where were you carrying them?'

'Where I always carried them— in a handkerchief round my neck.'

'Then you had two handkerchiefs with you when you returned to the ballroom?'

'Yes.'

'You say that while reciting the rosary, a peace came over you. Why didn't you then throw away your revolver?'

'I forgot all about it.'

'When did you remember it?'

'When it went off.'

'You did not remember that you had it until then?'

'No.'

Hubert Parker wasn't buying this story. And so followed a testy exchange with the accused.

Parker asked Audrey if she could show the courtroom how the handkerchief had been wrapped around the gun. She couldn't quite remember.

'It is rather difficult to conceal,' Parker said.

'No it isn't,' Audrey replied.

'How did you carry your rosary to the cathedral?'

Audrey told him she had rolled it into a handkerchief inside her dress.

'Tell me how you counted your rosary beads with one hand while holding the revolver in your other hand.'

'It was quite easy. The revolver was in my right hand and the beads in my left hand. It is easy to count the beads—one for each prayer.'

'With which hand did you touch Gidley on the shoulder?'

'The left hand.'

'Are you left-handed?'

'No.'

'Would not the natural impulse be to touch him with the right hand?'

'No.'

'Was it because you had the revolver in your right hand that you used your left?'

'No.'

'You had nothing against him until he said to you, "Pardon me—I'm dancing"?'

'No.'

'When he said those words something went snap in your head?'

'I was not myself. It was the shock of it all.'

'But don't forget,' Parker said, 'that you were at peace with the world by this time, and had forgiven him everything. Did you shoot him because of a snub?'

'No.'

'Or a slight?'

'No.'

'Or an insult?'

'No. The revolver went off accidentally.'

'You do not suggest that you were insane at the moment, do you?'

'No.'

'It was purely an accident?'

'Yes.'

'Your engagement to Gidley was broken off, was it not?'

'No, certainly not.'

'Gidley never wished to break it off?'

'No.'

'You never heard that he wanted it broken off?'

'No.'

'You agreed that it be announced to the public that it was broken off?'

'Yes, I agreed, to please him.'

'That was the only reason?'

'Yes.'

Arthur Haynes now re-examined his client, asking her about the commander she had known on the sloop. Audrey responded that he was fifty years of age and that they were 'merely friendly and never improper'. All of the ships' officers she had known had been friendly and respectful to her.

'A suggestion—a very improper one—was made by the Crown Prosecutor that something was found in your bag, and that your parents communicated with the police regarding the discovery. Now, what was found in your bag?'

'Only my rosary beads. My mother is a Protestant and my father is an atheist and has no time for any Church, least of all the Roman Catholic Church. He is dead against Roman Catholics.'

Parker shook his head in disbelief. He had read policewoman Chipper's report. Jessie Jacob had not found rosary beads in Audrey's bag. It was a condom. But Parker let it go.

It was now for Haynes to call the policewoman who had been with Audrey since she was taken into custody.

Policewoman Helen Dugdale took the stand and explained that she was with the accused for five hours after she was brought to the lock-up. Dugdale did not think Audrey was mentally fit to make a statement to police that day. She appeared to be a loving and trusting girl and did not strike her as callous or cold-blooded.

Hubert Parker stepped up to ask his own questions.

'The accused was quite rational, was she not?'

'She was worried.'

'Yes, of course, she was worried but was she sensible?'

'She was very worried.'

'Yes, yes, but was she rational?'

'Yes.'

'Quite a lot of the women with whom you come into contact in the course of your duties seem to be lovable, do they not although they are really bad lots?'

'That is the case with some of them. This girl is particularly lovable and gentle.'

It was, in fact, a strong show of support from a woman who had seen a lot of different girls and women in her line of work. And there were certainly some for whom she would not have given a favourable character reference.

Arthur Haynes called other witnesses, including Lewis Cunningham, licensee of the Leederville Hotel, who had been at the Government House ball. He saw Audrey being led away by the police. In his opinion she seemed to be unconcerned and unconscious of her surroundings, even trance-like.

Russell Sandeman, a press reporter, also gave evidence. He had been standing at the centre of the ballroom and saw Audrey walking towards Cyril and his dancing partner. She touched him on the left shoulder and he turned round, remarking, 'I'm dancing; I'll see you later,' or something to that effect. She raised her right arm and there was a report. Sandeman did not think that Audrey had taken aim.

Arthur Haynes then asked, 'Can you express an opinion as to whether the shooting was accidental or deliberate?'

Hubert Parker was quick to object. 'He can state facts. He cannot express an opinion.'

'Oh, no! Because you don't like it,' Haynes replied.

It was the judge's turn now to interject: 'Of course he does not like it. The question is an improper one.'

Haynes asked Russell Sandeman about Audrey's demeanour after the shooting and said she appeared to be 'quiet and dumbfounded'.

'So were you, were you not?'

'No.'

'Then, why didn't you take the revolver from her?'

'I thought it might go off again and a bullet hit someone else.'

'So you went for a policeman?'

'Yes. I told a friend to take the revolver from her, but he said he felt sick.'

Audrey's parents took the stand next. It was not easy for Jessie Jacob. She had already spoken publicly of her family's troubles and now she had to go through it all again, for the sake of her daughter.

Jessie confirmed that she had first met Cyril Gidley in May, or June, of 1924. Whenever Cyril's ship was in port, he was a frequent visitor to the Jacob house. One night, after Audrey had been out with Cyril, her mother found her crying in her bedroom and saw marks on her shoulder. Jessie spoke about the turmoil of her daughter leaving and coming back, Cyril sending threatening letters, and the on-again off-again engagement. Audrey had written to her mother from Perth asking for a revolver and Jessie had sent one up (there was another one in the house belonging to one of her sons) and it was always loaded.

Jessie also confirmed for Arthur Haynes that it was in fact a string of rosary beads she had found in Audrey's bag and was surprised by this, given her own Presbyterian faith. She told her husband she had found something in Audrey's bag but not what it was, for fear he would be annoyed.

The judge then asked Jessie: 'Do you wish to tell the jury that you informed your husband you had found something in the bag, but did not say what it was?'

'I did not tell him what it was.'

'Then what was the point of saying anything at all?'

'I was upset.'

Arthur Haynes asked Jessie about her daughter. 'Is your daughter flighty?'

'No. She has always been a hard-working girl.'

Hubert Parker cross-examined Audrey's mother. 'Why was the revolver given to her?'

'For her protection.'

Judge Northmore wanted to know why: 'Protection against what?'

'For her use, if necessary, when she was left in charge of the children.'

This was an interesting state of affairs but Hubert Parker pressed forward. 'You sent it up to your daughter two days before the *Kangaroo* left Fremantle?'

Jessie said she had.

'In view of the facts that Gidley had seduced your daughter, caught her by the throat, told you lies and induced your daughter to leave home and live under an assumed name, did not your opinion of him change?'

'Yes, of course it did.'

'And yet you arranged clandestine appointments between your daughter and Gidley?'

9. 'IN THE SHADOW OF THE GALLOWS'

'I was afraid of him, as he had threatened to kill my husband. I did not know what to do.'

'Your daughter has a bad temper, has she not?'

'No. She may be a bit hasty, but she puts up with more than most people would.'

'She objects to your husband being an atheist?'

'No.'

'Is he an atheist?'

'He doesn't believe in any church, but he's not an atheist.'

And yet, Audrey had said he was.

Victor Courtney also gave evidence for the defence. He had attended the ball at Government House and heard the report of the revolver. He saw a man lying on the floor and a crowd gather around him. His attention went to the accused, whom, he claimed, said nothing and was removed from the scene by a policeman. She had said for them to 'take me away quietly'. He testified that in in her right hand was a revolver, partly concealed by something white: 'She had a detached expression, and seemed unconscious of her surroundings.'

Hubert Parker asked Courtney if he should have taken the revolver from the accused to which the witness responded it was not his duty.

'Did you not think that she might have shot others?'

'There were others closer to her than I was, and I thought it might be dangerous to take it from her.'

Edward Jacob, Audrey's father, was called next. He confirmed he was an assistant clerk of courts at Fremantle and first heard of his daughter's engagement in October 1924. He was staying at a boarding house and was introduced to a 'Mr Douglas' and it was a while before he discovered this was Cyril Gidley. He didn't like Cyril at all, once it was revealed who he was, and thought it was a frame-up that Cyril was sidelining him from his family while he was involved with them. Gidley had gloated that he had it under control. Edward then tried in various ways to prevent Cyril from seeing his daughter. His wife also told him she found something in Audrey's bag but would not say what it was.

Hubert Parker asked questions about some of the incidents that had taken place. Edward 'did not remember a pie dish being broken over his head by the accused. A dish was thrown at him, but he did not know whether it came from the accused or from his wife.' He did, however, state that his separation from his wife was caused by Gidley's 'defamatory statements concerning his relations with other women'.

Hubert Parker asked: 'Regarding your relations with women, there was a big stir at Boulder once, and articles with flaring headlines appeared in the local newspapers, did they not?'

'Yes, but the stories were untrue, nothing but scandal.'

'And at Collie?'

'Something was said there.'

'About your relations with women?'

'Yes, but it was all spite. Nothing was true.'

Parker was trying to show that Cyril Gidley had been right about Edward Jacob and that he wasn't the one who was breaking the family apart. The marriage was already crumbling.

'Your separation was on account of a complaint of cruelty?'

'Yes.'

'And you are in charge of the files relating to such matters at Fremantle. The file concerning your case is missing?'

'What is missing?'

'The original complaint, unfortunately. Did any of your sons have a revolver?'

'Not at home, as far as I know.'

'Is it not a fact that unfortunate domestic difference had arisen between you and your wife from time to time?'

'No. There was never any serious trouble till Gidley came on the scene.'

'Never?'

'No. There were tiffs, but they were not serious.'

And as the newspapers reported, upon replying to further questions, Edward Jacob 'denied that on one occasion his wife had thrown a brick through his window'.

Arthur Haynes asked about the complaints made between Jessie and Edward Jacob. Edward responded: 'Exact copies of the complaint, involved in the separation proceedings were made in the charge book and in the Magistrate's record book at the Fremantle courthouse.'

The defence now closed its case with a startling statement. Arthur Haynes addressed the jury and told them this was a case which 'shrieked' for the application of 'the unwritten law'. This was a law in Europe, particularly France, where a defence could be made for a revenge killing. In the final stages of the defence's case, Audrey was now being portrayed as a woman who had killed her ex-lover because he had assaulted her.

The judge was less convinced: 'There is no unwritten law. I will ask the jury to observe their oaths.'

Arthur Haynes then said, aiming his point at the jury: 'I presume juries in other countries uphold their oaths, and, notwithstanding the written law, there have been cases similar to this where accused has been acquitted.'

To argue for the application of the unwritten law was a bold move by the defence.

Hubert Parker had already done his best in his closing address to throw off an emphasis on the unwritten law. Parker reminded the jury of what simply did not stack up in the evidence presented by the defence. Not only was Cyril Gidley unable to refute the allegations made against him but there were questions about Audrey's actions on the night of the shooting. The route Audrey had taken to the river to apparently take her own life was the wrong direction. The handkerchief used to cover the gun had never been seen by police before the trial. Parker claimed Arthur Haynes had introduced it in court as a device to put the jury off. There was no evidence beyond the statement of mother and daughter to suggest Cyril had seduced Audrey but, even if he had, Audrey had also told the courtroom she had forgiven Cyril. The evidence was clear. Audrey had shot Cyril with no provocation. If the members of the jury were worried about condemning a young woman to death, they needn't have. Parker explained that he had prosecuted other cases involving young women and that they had been spared execution but had been held accountable for their crimes.

Justice Northmore closed the proceedings by summing up the evidence and reminding the jury they were not here to consider

Cyril's character. The dead man could not speak for himself nor could anyone properly speak on his behalf. There were three verdicts which the jury could decide on. Manslaughter was not one of them because it would have had to have been shown that Cyril had been shot in a moment of provocation or 'heat of passion'. The jury could, however, reach a verdict of wilful murder if they believed the evidence showed Audrey had planned to kill Cyril. Murder could also be decided if she had intended to inflict grievous bodily harm. The last option open to the twelve men of the jury was a verdict of not guilty.

The jury retired at six that evening and the accused, the lawyers and the press waited for a verdict with bated breath.

The jurors had a serious task ahead of them. Would they be swayed by the arguments made by Arthur Haynes, particularly that Audrey had accidentally shot Cyril and had been led into this situation through his persistent cruelty? Or would they follow more of the police and prosecution line of thinking that Audrey shot Cyril because she was a jilted lover who wanted revenge? There was the evidence that Audrey had threatened Cyril's life but the defence lawyer created some doubt around the authenticity of the letter. And that might be all that was needed: doubt cast over the evidence presented.

The jury returned with a verdict in less than three hours. Hubert Parker and Arthur Haynes took up their positions and Audrey waited in the dock. There were no indications as to how this would play out but it seemed more of a certainty that Audrey would be found guilty. She must have known it herself.

Judge Northmore addressed the jury and asked for their verdict.

The colour drained from Audrey's face. Reporters watched as she started to tremble. She looked on the verge of collapse.

The young woman stared straight ahead as the verdict was read out.

'Not guilty.'

9. 'IN THE SHADOW OF THE GALLOWS'

It took her a few moments to react. Then she fell into the arms of two policewomen with her in the dock.

There was a moment of silence and then a gasp came from 'all parts of the court'. Then almost immediately there was applause. Men and women clapped in the public gallery. There were cheers and even some screams. All decorum had been lost and Judge Northmore worked hard to restore it but eventually gave up.

Audrey was led down to her mother, who wrapped her in a hug, and together they watched as the floor of the court filled with people. The barristers in their wigs and gowns were surprised by the reaction, watching as people tried to get close to shake hands with Audrey, to congratulate her, or simply get a closer look at her.

Led out of the building by her parents, smiling, trying not to cry, Audrey looked overcome. Edward and Jessie Jacob were emotional too, knowing they were finally taking their daughter home. Audrey, her parents, and her lawyer walked through and past cheering onlookers. Some of Audrey's friends were there too and jostled to hug her.

Victor Courtney, editor of the *Mirror* newspaper, was there to congratulate Audrey and was granted the story he had wanted for the last few weeks. His favourable reports had certainly influenced the public's perception of Audrey and he had earned the right to secure the first interview with Audrey Jacob.

'I—I can't quite realise anything!' Audrey Jacob told Victor, who would later write it up as a significant moment for a 'free girl once again' entering back into the outside world.

While he listened to Audrey, Victor Courtney was already putting the story together in his head: 'In the great crises of people's lives, even minutes bring marvellous changes'. He would put those last two words in block letters for better emphasis. Her excitement was in contrast to the nervous young woman who had just been inside the courtroom, waiting for the verdict: 'Her lips were tightly drawn, her eyes strained and tired-looking, her whole attitude something akin to nervous prostration.'

'What were your first thoughts when you heard the jury's verdict?' Victor asked.

'Well, just as the jury came in, I had caught a glimpse of mother's face, and I'll never forget how it looked. My first thought was to go to her. Well, it seemed as if the next instant I was down those awful steps and in her arms, and I heard the clapping and the cheering, and everybody was wanting to shake hands.'

The strain of the wait was hard: 'Yes, the six weeks of it was bad enough but the last hours after the jury retired I—', Audrey clasped her hands nervously, that's how he would write it—

> 'I don't think I'll ever forget it. It was mostly silence where I was, but I could hear now and again a laugh or a scrap of talk from outside, and somehow that made me feel all the more miserable. Yes, I think to-day has been the worst time of all, but those few seconds from the time I went back into the dock until the time the foreman spoke were worse than the whole six weeks. Oh—I, don't want to talk about them!'

Victor asked her about the 'demonstrations of sympathy in court' and Audrey smiled, replying, 'I think the people are something wonderful. After all, what did it matter to them what happened to me? They didn't know me, and I don't think I'd have blamed them if they'd have judged me wrong. But for perfect strangers to come and shake hands with me, and for women to come and kiss me as they did tonight—I think it was wonderful Christian-like.'

And then she pleaded with Victor: 'Please, if you want to say anything, say how much I appreciate all this and how I thank them.'

Would she be staying in Perth? the seasoned journalist asked, thinking of what his readers would want to know.

'Well, everybody has been so kind to me that I now feel I would like to stay here. At present my idea is to go on with my painting and to try and save sufficient money to open a studio.'

'Is there anything else you want to say?'

'Yes, I want to say how kind everybody has been to me both at Fremantle Prison and the Perth lock-up, and I will never forget Mrs Dugdale's kindness. She has helped me to bear up all through. And then, of course, I owe my liberty in great measure to the efforts put forward on my behalf by my counsel, Mr Haynes. For the last two or three weeks he gave up everything else to concentrate on my case. Right from the first he told me the ultimate verdict would be "Not guilty," but it has been an anxious ordeal for me. He, however, never for one moment lost confidence, and this is what has principally helped me to keep my spirits up.'

Victor pushed Audrey further about her plans for the future, and her thoughts seemed to have shifted.

'I don't know as yet. My first thoughts were that if I succeeded in establishing my innocence, I would like to go away from everything and everybody—somewhere where nobody would ever know me.'

And then Audrey was thinking once more about her freedom, and with this smiled at Victor: 'You know, I have been so used to the bare prison walls during the last six weeks of the prison routine, I can hardly realise I am free. Tomorrow it will be a case of breakfast in bed, instead of having to follow the wardress out of my cell.'

Audrey shook Victor's hand and turned away, towards her parents. Victor would later use powerful journalistic prose to secure further sympathy for Audrey: 'With only 20 years of life, she has surely had a terrible sequence of experiences, and a crowd of memories that a hundred normal lives would not register.'

Even as Audrey was taken away in a car, the cheers could still be heard.

There was no precedent for what had just happened. Perth had never seen a case like it. The prosecution argued she was a jilted lover who had wilfully shot Cyril Gidley. It should have been an open-and-shut guilty verdict. But Arthur Haynes had successfully argued a defence case that Audrey had been seduced and abandoned by Cyril and thus had the right to take her revenge. He had called on the application of the 'unwritten law'. The jury had accepted his argument that Audrey had accidentally shot Cyril, overcome in that moment by the emotions of his cruelty.

Support for Audrey continued beyond the Supreme Court grounds. One person, writing to Victor Courtney at the *Mirror*, believed it was 'up to us to give the girl a chance to make good'. Knowing that Audrey wanted to open a painting studio, the writer of the letter—'SPORT'—enclosed '£5 towards the expense, and would like you to agree to receive subscriptions from others'. The newspaper duly acknowledged it would receive further 'subscriptions' towards getting Audrey a studio.

It was a dramatic end to a case that had captured the interest of the city and the nation. Audrey Jacob was a free woman.

Edward Cutting, the Murphys and others who had known Cyril Gidley left the Supreme Court unable to comprehend what had just happened. What had seemed a straightforward case had turned into something else entirely. The reaction to the verdict had been almost euphoric. Cyril's friends found themselves surrounded by people cheering in support of the woman who shot Cyril dead.

It was hardest for Edward Cutting. Not only had he known Cyril in life and then had to identify him in death, he had been communicating with the Gidley family back in England. What was he going to tell them now? If any of the newspaper stories reached them back in England, it would be even worse than hearing the verdict. They would hear about the celebrations in the courtroom and the fanfare surrounding Audrey as she departed with her friends and parents. Edward was left trying to equate the man he had known with the person the defence lawyer had portrayed in court. It didn't measure up. Cyril had been a bit of a lad enjoying the attentions of some young women but Edward hadn't expected the evidence that had been presented about Cyril terrorising Audrey and her family. All the same, Audrey had shot his friend dead and yet had been acquitted of the crime. It was baffling.

It was little better for Crown Prosecutor Hubert Parker. He left the courtroom in stunned disbelief. He knew Haynes was good at his job but how had Audrey got off with murder? What could he have done differently with the case? Should he have pushed questions about her

9. 'IN THE SHADOW OF THE GALLOWS'

lifestyle more? Could the police have found more people to testify on Cyril's behalf?

There would be no closure for Cyril Gidley's family, only the same sense of incredulity. Through the help of Cyril's friend, Edward Cutting, and the lawyers in Perth, Cyril's personal belongings were sent back to his family in England. According to the list prepared by the police and signed off by the Commissioner of Police, these personal effects were:

2 Suit cases containing clothing & personal effects.
2 Canvas kit bags.
1 Tool box.
1 Bag containing Tortoise shell.
1 Motor cycle.
1 Leather kit bag.

Along with a rug there was another bundle which really brought home the reality of what had happened to their son: '2 Bundles of clothing worn by deceased on night of 27th August, 1925.'

Joseph Gidley also requested that his son's letter of 16 August 1925 be sent to the family. But because this evidence was used by the prosecution to show Audrey had threatened Cyril's life, and was still being held as an exhibit in the Supreme Court, the item was not sent. Inspector Stephen Condon wrote to the Commissioner of Police that he did not think it was 'advisable to part with it'. It's not clear why Cyril's parents wanted the letter but perhaps it offered them an opportunity to keep a record of what they believed to be the truth of the case against what felt very much like an unjust verdict.

10. 'I told him everything'

Jubilant as she was at her acquittal, Audrey soon realised she needed a break from Perth. Gossip and news travelled quickly and her face had been splashed across all the major newspapers. There would be few anonymous trips to the harbour and port for Audrey now. Reporters were still keen to find out what was in store for Audrey and her family, so even the family home was no safe haven.

Jessie Jacob's Junner family in Melbourne were keen to help Audrey out. It was the Junners after all who had assisted with some of her legal costs. So, in early December, Audrey was onboard a boat, sailing for a new life in Melbourne. In her personal belongings, Audrey carried a letter of introduction from her lawyer, Arthur Haynes, to one of his other clients, forty-one-year-old Jack De Garis. As Audrey would soon find out, it was an interesting introduction for Haynes to give her.

Born in 1884, Clement John ('Jack') De Garis was Melbourne-born but the family business in dried fruits was in Mildura, over five hundred kilometres north-west of the city. Jack managed the business in his late teens and by the age of twenty-one was in charge of the Mildura business. He was a charming, energetic man and by 1907, as business boomed, he had married and went on to have three daughters. But Jack De Garis was an entrepreneur with grand ideas

10. 'I TOLD HIM EVERYTHING'

which he hoped would take him across the country and around the world.

De Garis' first venture saw him borrow thousands of pounds to set up a packing shed and then in 1913, after raising more money, he bought ten thousand acres in South Australia. He moved a staff of eighty into cottages on the property, and expanded his fruiting business. The business venture saw De Garis also provide valuable services for his employees on the property, such as a school and library. His Sunraysed fruiting business continued to expand through World War One.

But Jack De Garis was more than just a dried-fruits man. He ventured into the arts, establishing a novel competition and wrote a musical comedy. It was a flop when launched in Perth, with most of the audience also realising it was publicised along with flyers and posters for De Garis' fruit business. The failure didn't keep De Garis down for long; he turned to aviation as his next venture. Remarkably, he claimed a number of interstate flying records. Next, he decided to create a fifty-thousand-acre settlement on Kendenup, the former property of the Hassell family in Western Australia. He moved there in 1921 and brought over three hundred people with him to work on the property.

Then the tide turned. Jack De Garis' family life disintegrated. He divorced his wife in 1923 and shortly after married his former private secretary. There were accusations Jack was on the verge of bankruptcy, made by a man he had exposed as a fraud. Though the claims were dismissed, Kendenup was losing more money than Jack could afford, given he was still paying the loans. He travelled to the United States to raise more funds, which were promised but never eventuated. He tried to raise money from real estate and another failed venture drilling for oil on the Mornington Peninsula.

Things fell apart quickly. On 5 January 1925, Jack De Garis wrote seventy farewell letters, telling family, friends and business associates he was going to take his life by drowning in Port Phillip Bay. Instead, he took off to New Zealand where he was arrested a week later. He was cleared of fraud charges later that year, represented by none other than

Arthur Haynes. The whole tale could very well have come straight out of a book—and indeed, De Garis put pen to paper and tried to make something of his forty years for a wider audience.

Published only weeks before the infamous ballroom shooting in Perth, Jack De Garis' novel, *Victories of Failure,* was his grandiose effort to share his experiences under the guise of the protagonist Kenneth Rogers in a 'business romance' tale. The foreword reads: 'This is the romance of a man who failed twice—once badly, and once very badly.' The only thing separating De Garis from the book was the different names used. The story travails the many different ventures of his life, from Mildura to Kendenup, and the business failures that led to his downfall. But the newspapers publicising the release of the book were optimistic this enterprising businessman could rise again.

Just what Arthur Haynes had planned in trying to connect Audrey with Jack De Garis is unclear but Audrey joined De Garis' social circle and enjoyed many parties in her new home town. She was often seen at the De Garis house in St Kilda, socialising with new Melbourne friends. It was in the hustle and bustle of this new social world that Audrey met her future husband on Boxing Day 1925.

Forty-nine-year-old Roger Duncan Sinclair was a clean-shaven, confident and charismatic American businessman. He was a director and one of the shareholders in the General Electric Company and though he worked a great deal in New York City, he kept a large home in Schenectady in New York State. This meant he was a wealthy bachelor already catching the eye of many women around Melbourne's social scene. He had been in Australia for a few months already, on business, before meeting Audrey at a party in St Kilda.

It was a whirlwind romance. Roger proposed to Audrey soon after their first meeting and less than three weeks later, on 12 January 1926, they were wed at the Registrar's Office at 165 Collins Street, Melbourne. Norman Anderson, consul with the US Consulate in Melbourne, was there to provide the Sinclairs with a consulate record of their marriage, affirming its legal status for Roger as an American citizen.

It was later presumed that Roger gave Audrey a pearl necklace as a wedding present and she would be seen wearing it in the weeks

10. 'I TOLD HIM EVERYTHING'

ahead as they set off on the next chapter of their lives together. Not long after they had said their vows, she and Roger boarded a ship taking them away from Melbourne and eventually on to America. Another gift was his surname. It would give Audrey more anonymity.

But Audrey was not out of the spotlight just yet. Only days before meeting her future husband, St Kilda—the place where Audrey had planned to set up a new life—was rocked by a horrific murder and Audrey was once again in the press, implicated in another murder case.

On 15 December 1925, sixty-five-year-old Henry Tacke confronted Frederick Currell as he slept on a bed on the porch of his St Kilda home. Henry was angry because he had been contributing to the upkeep of the Currell family home and he felt that Frederick's wife, Rachel, did not appreciate it. Rachel had been working in a secretarial capacity for Henry and he had bought her a number of gifts, as well as loaning her money. Frederick told Henry they should take the argument indoors so as not to draw attention to themselves from neighbours hearing the argument. As they walked inside the house, Henry Tacke hit Frederick Currell on the back of the head, knocking his hat off, and as Frederick turned, he saw Henry pull something from his pocket. Henry fired a shot at Frederick but missed. The bullet hit Rachel Currell in the darkened hallway. Henry fired a number of other shots into the hallway. Henry Tacke took off, leaving Rachel Currell, a mother of five, dead on the floor from the five bullets that had hit her.

Henry Tacke was found by police hiding out on the beach at Sorrento. He claimed it had been an accident and his intention had been to use the gun to take his own life. As police would find out, Henry Tacke and Rachel Currell were reportedly having an affair.

Following the story closely, Perth's *Truth* newspaper reported that an American couple had been paying for cigarettes and other goods to be sent to Tacke in prison. They went by the names of Mr and Mrs Clifford Clarke. There was great speculation about who they were. Sensationally, the newspaper claimed that when a photograph of Audrey and Roger Sinclair was shown to two people who had seen the couple visit Tacke in prison, they thought they were the Clarkes. There was no evidence pointing to this actually being the case, and questions surrounded whether the newspaper was falsely trying to link Audrey to another murder case.

Nevertheless, Tacke's defence was quite similar to Audrey's. He said he had been provoked into killing his lover but could not remember any of the attack. But there the similarity with Audrey's case ended. Tacke was found guilty of manslaughter and received seven years in prison. He died eighteen months later from blood poisoning.

Newlywed Audrey Sinclair returned to Fremantle in January 1926, keen to introduce Roger to her family before they continued on to the United States. It was not the quiet homecoming that she might have hoped for. Soon after, amid speculation that she was back in town, she gave an interview to *Truth* newspaper from her washtub where she apparently had been found in the act of doing her washing. She wiped the lather from her hands onto the apron covering her white working frock.

'Gee! Sandy, I'm right glad to see you, Shake,' she said to the *Truth* reporter her mother had let into the house. Jessie Jacob and the younger children were still in the High Street house in Fremantle. 'Come right inside and sit down. I was just trying to do a little washing whilst the boat is in port; so you will excuse me.'

'We entered the little old one-storied brick villa at 592 High-street, Fremantle, that loomed so largely in the public eye just five months ago, and we sat down,' the reporter would later type. 'I looked at her and wondered. So this gay, laughing girl whom I last saw with pale, drawn face and an expression of fear in her eyes, in the Criminal dock at the Supreme Court in Perth in October last was Audrey Jacob. I was a witness at the trial.'

10. 'I TOLD HIM EVERYTHING'

The reporter was none other than Russell Sandeman, a witness at the inquest and trial, and now anxious for the latest update about the acquitted accused in Perth's most sensational murder trial. Audrey couldn't be happier to see him, or so the reporter would claim for *Truth* readers: 'Audrey was not a bit abashed. Washtub or no washtub. She wanted to tell me her life story; that is, her life since the killing of Cyril Gidley.'

Audrey explained to the reporter that it had all been a hideous nightmare and that she had lived for Cyril, the man she loved. And then the nightmare had started. But now, she said as she finished drying her hands, she had fallen in love again, at first sight.

'Well, Sandy, I suppose you want me to tell you everything. How I met Roger? What I did before I met him. And what I have done since I have met him?' And then playfully she said, laughing, 'I can't tell you everything of our life together, but believe me, Roger is some boy.'

Even though she had only known Roger a short period of time, Audrey was already sounding a little like the American wife, according to what Sandy was putting together in his head. She told him she needed him to 'get this straight'.

'We do not want publicity, Roger and I, but I feel that I would like to tell you something of what I have been doing.'

'That suits me,' Sandy replied, 'for that is what I came to see you about.'

And so, Audrey told it all after all these weeks.

'Well after that dreadful nightmare, when Cyril Gidley was killed, I left, presumably to go to Sydney, but I did not do so. I got to Melbourne, and decided, to stay at my relatives. Whilst there—in Melbourne I mean—I met my old friend Jack De Garis—you know, C. J. De Garis —and he gave me some wonderful times. I went out to his home, and had parties in galore. It was one glorious time. I lived [sic?] every minute of it.'

And then she met Roger Sinclair and fell in love.

'I did not meet him at Jack De Garis' place, as has been implied. I met him at a swell party at St Kilda on Boxing night, and, as I told you before, I fell in love with him at first sight. He was living at Menzies Hotel and he made an appointment to see me again. He, too, was interested. I had thought of returning to Perth to open up a studio and get back to my artistic work, but Roger told me that he loved me, and he wanted me to marry him. This did not trouble me at all, because I wanted to marry him, but as I was only twenty, and not twenty-two as people thought, I was worried. So we talked the matter over, and I wrote to my mother asking her consent to the marriage. Meanwhile, Roger went to Sydney on business for his firm. You know, he is with the General Electric Company of America, which has its head office in New York. My mother had a terrible job with my father to get him to consent to the marriage, but, finally, dad agreed, and I sent word to Roger and he booked by the *Demosthenes* for Durban. He booked for me, too, you know, because we had decided to get married when he returned to Melbourne, if I got my parents' consent. He came back by the *Demosthenes*, and we went to the office of a Registrar of Marriages … Roger, dear boy, insisted upon paying the Registrar double the ordinary fee. Lots of people will tell you that my husband is wealthy, and you might think he is, too, by this instance of throwing money away, but I can tell you that even I did not know how wealthy he is until after I married him.'

'Did Mr Sinclair know all about the Gidley tragedy?' Sandy asked.

'Oh, yes,' Audrey replied, 'he knew all about that. I told him everything but it did not trouble him at all. It worried both of us, however, to avoid publicity in Melbourne, and, therefore after the marriage, he left Menzies Hotel, and we went to Carlyon's Hotel, at St Kilda, to live.

'Quite a lot of people at St Kilda thought that they knew me and kept asking questions as to who I was before marriage. We gave them false names. Their curiosity was aroused because of the publicity given to my trial, and then when I got to Melbourne, and was taken about by the De Garises, a number of men wanted to marry me…'

And then Audrey shared how her father had tried to stop the wedding but it had been too late by that stage.

Pressed on her future plans, Audrey was firm in wanting to start a new life, and that she had no wish to return to Australia: 'No. My husband might, but I am going away to live a quiet and peaceful life and have a good time.'

But all was not as it seemed in this fairytale romance, according to one young Melburnian. He wrote to *Truth* newspaper in January

10. 'I TOLD HIM EVERYTHING'

to tell them of his relationship with Audrey which overlapped with her romance and engagement to Roger Sinclair. He included a letter Audrey had sent him, written from her residence at 'Mignon', 42 Robe Street, St Kilda:

> Dear—
>
> What is the matter with you? You have not rang me for days. Surely you have not forgotten me already. I can't ring you, as I have not your 'phone number. Would you please give it to me? And when are you coming out to see me? Don't forget to let me know, so that I will be at home.
>
> I am having a wonderful time, and will be really sorry when my holiday comes to an end, but that is always the way when one begins to enjoy themself; it is always time to go back home. It was a great Christmas for me, and I sincerely hope you enjoyed it as much as I did.
>
> This kind of weather is splendid, and the water is beautiful. Carl and I go down every morning. We would not miss our little swim for anything. Last Wednesday we went for a little trip down the bay to Queenscliff. I have another aunt living there, and she is a real sport, too. We are going down to Queenscliff again next week for a few days, and hope to have a good time. We have invitations to a big ball that is being held there.
>
> I don't suppose you have any letters for me, otherwise I would have surely heard from you sooner. Well, don't forget to 'phone me or write a few lines.
>
> Cheerio, with kind regards and the compliments of the season from
>
> Yours sincerely, "AUDREY."

The letter was dated 2 January, only two weeks before Audrey married Roger. And then, on 15 January, Audrey wrote again, this time from Carlyon's Hotel in St Kilda, to tell this man that she was married. She described her husband as a wealthy American and they were going to be leaving on the Saturday for New York, via London.

With yet another scandal following Audrey, she and Roger stuck to their plans to leave Australia. They left on the *Demosthenes* on 21 January, not long after Audrey's *Truth* interview, headed for New York. They hoped that the past might be forgotten and that they could start a new life in the United States, free of the attention that had followed them to Melbourne and back to Fremantle.

Word got back to Fremantle, however, that Audrey had fallen into some serious trouble again, and this time it was not of her own doing. The port city gossip detailed how she was now stranded and penniless in South Africa. Her wealthy husband had proved too good to be true and now, scandalously revealed as a bigamist, he had deserted Audrey, leaving her completely alone. She was appealing to her friends and family to send funds to help her return to Australia.

Victor Courtney heard the rumours and was quick to dispel them. Audrey's old ally at the *Mirror* newspaper had been receiving letters from her and he checked in with her mother to see if there was any truth to the rumours. In a July 1926 article, Courtney openly objected to the latest spate of rumours. The *Mirror* could find no truth in the stranded stories, nor that Audrey's husband was a bigamist.

By her own letters to Victor Courtney, Audrey told of her travels from Fremantle to South Africa, and then on to London where they had stayed at the glamorous Waldorf Hotel. Audrey became very unwell with the flu and 'for some time caused her husband and the doctors some anxiety'. Once Audrey was well again, the couple left for New York and had reached Boston early in May. They would eventually settle into a home in Connecticut. Audrey wrote to her mother soon after, telling her of her safe arrival on American shores and how her husband was showing her great 'kindness and attention'.

Victor Courtney hoped these details from letters would 'dispel the fanciful story of her stranding in Africa'. He also expressed concern at the pain such rumours would cause for Audrey's family. There were many who had wished her well when she left and the editor hoped this would continue. Putting the gravity of what Audrey had been involved in less than a year before, the editor asked that Audrey be given a chance: 'Why cannot people give it to her?'

10. 'I TOLD HIM EVERYTHING'

For, in spite of a press keen to sniff out a scandal, Audrey *had* been given another chance. Cyril Gidley knew no more than his twenty-five years. In August 1926, marking the anniversary of his death, Cyril's parents had a notice inserted in the *West Australian* for their 'dear son'. 'His was a promising life', the notice read, and was followed by remembrances from the *Kangaroo* engineers for 'our dear shipmate and comrade'. Friends, too, remembered a 'dear friend'.

✦ ✦ ✦

Audrey moved to the United States with her husband to set up a new life—but what of those whose lives continued in Western Australia?

Edward and Jessie did not live long after the trial. Edward Jacob died at Perth Hospital on 27 September 1928. He had been working away again as a clerk of courts, this time in Roebourne, before returning to Perth for medical treatment. Edward was memorialised as the 'beloved husband' of Jessie and a 'fond father'. He was fifty-five years old. Jessie Jacob died just seven months after her husband on 27 April 1929. Before being taken to Kareenya Hospital in the city, Jessie had been living at 904 Albany Road, Victoria Park. Jessie was fifty years old. The Jacobs were buried together in the same plot at Karrakatta Cemetery.

The ballroom shooting and subsequent trial must have taken its toll on Edward and Jessie Jacob. The defence case of trying to convince the jury of Audrey's ordeal at the hands of a manipulative, cruel lover rested on laying bare key details about Cyril's accusations against Edward Jacob. Their private lives were turned public through the courts and reported for anyone to read about, not just in Perth but across the country.

Hubert Parker resigned from the position of Crown Prosecutor in June 1926. He returned to his private legal practice but he didn't stay in it long. He became a Member of the Legislative Assembly for North-East Fremantle from 1930 to 1933 and, after a brief stint as attorney-general, served for two decades on the Legislative Council representing the Metropolitan-Suburban province. Parker also continued his association with the Returned Soldiers' League. He died in Shenton Park on 26 July 1966, aged eighty-two.

Detective Sergeant Joseph Frazer continued on in his role as head of the Fremantle CIB and would play a central role in another shocking case in 1929. On 30 September 1929, Robert Hall walked into the home of Mr and Mrs Hepburn on High Road, Palmyra. He shot and wounded them and their daughter, Jessie, before taking off a half mile up the road where next he shot a taxi driver while he slept in his bed. Hall fled into bushland while yet another victim was found shot dead near Preston Point Road. It wasn't long before Hall found himself surrounded by police, led by DS Frazer, and opted to take his own life. It was a horrific suburban shooting and murder spree and Frazer was commended for bringing it to an end. Frazer then went on to serve in Broome but came back to Fremantle in 1933 with a promotion to inspector. He took ill only a short while later and died at his home at 494 High Street, Fremantle on 13 June 1933. He had lived on the same street as the Jacob family. Fifty-nine-year-old Joseph Frazer was survived by his wife, Ella, and their four children.

Sergeant William Brodie retired from the police force in 1938 after having served for close to forty years. His colleague Alfred Timms who had also been on duty at the Government House ball, was celebrated in the years that followed for more than just his work. He was the 'singing detective' and 'musical bobby' known in the Police Band for his abilities both with instruments and his voice, which harkened back to his Welsh ancestry. He became a sergeant in the late 1920s and was an inspector by 1936. Outside his city work, he served at Broome and the wider Kimberley region. Timms retired from the force in November 1943, having served for forty-one years. He lived a quiet life and died in 1956 aged seventy-seven.

Arthur Haynes enjoyed a long legal career where he was noted for his wit, attention to detail and 'championing of the underdog'. But it was not without its controversies. In 1931 he was charged with having induced a witness to give false testimony. It was alleged Haynes had told a young female witness she could give false testimony in order to avoid scandal and controversy. In the context of the Audrey Jacob

10. 'I TOLD HIM EVERYTHING'

case, it was an interesting charge. In this case, Arthur faced Arthur Kidson once more as the resident magistrate sitting on the bench for the case.

Haynes had been representing a man charged with 'unlawful carnal knowledge of a girl'. It was alleged Haynes went to see the girl and tried to convince her to marry his client. A few days later, Arthur's old mate at the *Mirror* newspaper, Victor Courtney, was quick to run a celebratory piece that the charges against Haynes had been dismissed. The paper claimed there was cheering in the Police Court.

Along with his busy legal practice, Haynes worked with members of the Liberal Party and, though he never aspired to enter into politics, he was influential in shaping some of the party thinking. His son, Richard, joined him in the legal practice.

Arthur Haynes died on 19 September 1952, aged sixty-six. Over thirty of those years were spent as a barrister. The Audrey Jacob case still figured greatly in the public mind as reports were circulated about his funeral at Karrakatta Cemetery. The *Sunday Times* recalled his 'victory in securing the acquittal of Audrey Jacob', a case which 'created an Australia-wide sensation'.

A week after Haynes' death, ex-CIB Chief, Henry 'Harry' Mann, wrote a piece for the *Mirror* newspaper in which he declared the Audrey Jacob trial Haynes' 'greatest case':

> In all walks of life a man's work is often best appreciated by those who are in opposition to him. Lawyers can frequently give you the best appreciation of a detective's qualities and detectives can sum up the abilities of leading lawyers. In one of my duties I was frequently opposed to the late Arthur Haynes when he assumed so capably the mantle of his brilliant father the late R.S. Haynes, KC. Arthur Haynes was one of the most vigorous and devastating cross-examiners I have ever seen in action in this State and his legal knowledge was extensive and sound. His lamented death has set me recalling some of his many triumphs and although I was not professionally

engaged at the time I name his defence of Audrey Jacob as among his numerous victories in criminal trials. By sheer skill and ability he won acquittal and freedom for his client. [It is a] story still talked of when historic cases are discussed.

Harry Willoughby Mann had worked for many years in Perth's CIB, investigating some of the state's worst crimes. In his later years, after his retirement, Mann wrote a crime column for the *Mirror* newspaper and was often called on to give his professional insights into crime cases. Though he had retired from his job as a detective-inspector a few years before Cyril Gidley's death, the case remained an important one for Mann, when later reflecting in print on the passing of Haynes.

Harry Mann died only a short while after Arthur Haynes, on 4 October 1952, aged eighty-one.

By the 1960s, all the main players in the Audrey Jacob trial had passed away. Victor Courtney, the *Mirror* newspaper editor who had played an instrumental part in gaining public sympathy for the accused, died on 1 December 1970, aged seventy-six.

But one person remained alive all these years and they were the only one who really knew what had happened in the murder of Cyril Gidley.

11. '... probable heart attack'

For the last six years, a retired artist had been quietly living by herself in a small two-bedroom house at 2515 Herring Avenue, Waco, Texas. Her husband had died many years before in Los Angeles County, on 24 March 1944, aged sixty-seven. She had been widowed at the age of thirty-nine and never remarried. Their daughter, an only child, Vivienne, had made her mother very proud. She was born in California on 3 October 1934 and accepted into UCLA at the age of sixteen. Graduating with a Bachelors in Spanish, she went on to complete her Masters in Spanish American Literature. In the 1950s, she worked in US Air Force Intelligence and was responsible for transporting intelligence documents during the Cuban Crisis, armed with a pistol to protect herself. She would later serve a tour of duty in the Vietnam War.

On 5 November 1970, aged sixty-five, the retired artist suffered a 'probable heart attack' at home and died. On the death certificate, she was identified as Audrey Sinclair, wife of Roger, and daughter of Edward Campbell and Jessie Junner. There was no mention of the Jacob name but this was Audrey Jacob, dead in Texas forty-five years after the ballroom shooting in Perth. Why she was living in Texas is another of the mysteries of Audrey's life.

At the request of her family, Audrey's body was transported to Santa Barbara Cemetery. An inscription on the memorial plaque at that cemetery, which she shared with her husband, read 'There is no greater gift in all eternity than courage'. It was an interesting choice of inscription. What was its meaning to the Sinclairs? Audrey's details were first on the plaque, followed by Roger. If it was a new memorial Vivienne had created when her mother died, was she reflecting on her mother's courage from her earlier life—that she had come through a terrible ordeal and yet managed to escape the scandal and create a new life for herself in the United States? Perhaps Vivienne was the only person to really know what her mother had gone through and what she thought about it through the years.

Audrey's American life unfolded quietly on the other side of the world to Perth, where people could still recall the ballroom shooting. She had no plans to return to Australia, having become a naturalised American citizen in 1939. The new life she had tried to create in Melbourne in the months following the death of Cyril Gidley had not worked out, and it was only by being on the other side of the world that she could live a private life away from the media attention in Australia.

The Audrey Jacob murder trial is unique in Australian history. Not only were women in the early twentieth century less likely to commit violent crimes than men, but Arthur Haynes' defence using the 'unwritten law' was uncommon. Judge Northmore declared in court in response to Haynes that there was no 'unwritten law' in Australia. There were defence cases where abuse and violence was used to argue for mercy but Arthur Haynes was intent on showing that Audrey had been assaulted and abandoned and this was grounds for a revenge killing—'the unwritten law' that, as he told the courtroom, was applied in France and the United States.

Haynes also argued that it was an accidental shooting brought on by the act of Cyril ignoring Audrey and publicly slighting her. Audrey was in a daze when she returned to the ballroom and didn't know what she was doing. After walking to the river and deciding not to take her own life, Audrey returned to Government House but had forgotten about the revolver in her hand until it went off. All the months of the young man's abuse and terrorising of her family, and his trying to break up her parents' marriage culminated in that moment on the dancefloor, when Audrey just wanted Cyril to notice her, to speak to her, to at least acknowledge her existence.

Arthur Haynes' defence case was expertly put together, but we must not discount the fact that Audrey may have actually been sexually assaulted by Cyril. She could have suffered trauma from the evening when he 'seduced' her, as she detailed in her statement at the trial. She could have been an abused partner in a relationship where she loved Cyril and didn't want to leave him. She still had 'fond memories' of Cyril, as she told Hermann Goerling after the relationship was over. But the ball allowed the trauma to resurface when Audrey was confronted with her abuser enjoying the company of other women and ignoring her.

It would not have been easy for Audrey to admit in court to being sexually assaulted, especially as a young unmarried woman, and, by all accounts, she was deeply affected in relating what happened that night. But the question remains as to why her mother would have some knowledge of this and still continue to let her see Cyril. Was Jessie really worried about the threats from Cyril?

In practical terms, in 1925, there were few options for support for victims of sexual violence. Audrey could have gone to see one of the members of the Women Police but this might have felt as hard as going to see a doctor about what she had been through. Even today, when there are numerous avenues of support available, victims infrequently come forward immediately after an attack.

Arthur Haynes' ability to convince the jury also depended on Hubert Parker's Crown prosecution case. It was short by comparison to Haynes', with only five witnesses called for the prosecution, compared to the eighteen people Parker called at the coronial inquest. Was Parker so confident that Audrey would be found guilty—largely based on the indisputable fact she had shot Cyril in front of numerous witnesses—and so did not feel the need to present more witnesses? Cyril's uncle in New South Wales had even contacted the police by telegram to offer any help with their case. Why was he not brought over as a key character witness? He could have spoken to the allegations that Cyril had or had not been sent away from home to turn his life around. Why was policewoman Laura Chipper not called to give evidence about her meeting with Audrey's parents? The jury could have listened to a policewoman swear under oath that Jessie Jacob was worried about her daughter's lifestyle and had in fact found a condom in her daughter's bag. There appeared to be at least some evidence Parker could have brought to cast doubt on Audrey's character.

Much more could have been made by the prosecution of the note Cyril wrote a few days before he was shot, in which Cyril claimed Audrey had threatened his life, and that he was writing the note 'in case she does keep her vow'. The police could have used Cyril's will as evidence to match the handwriting when Arthur Haynes questioned its authenticity. Whatever the mystery of its sudden appearance on his bed, Cyril's will was created in April 1925 and the handwriting was the same as the writing in the note that claimed Audrey had threatened his life. This was an argument against accidental shooting. It showed that Audrey was unstable and had thought about harming Cyril before the Government House ball. But the prosecution case was not built around this piece of evidence and Haynes was able to discredit it by casting doubt over its legitimacy.

The prosecution did not also delve into the matter of the address book and diary apparently stolen from Audrey's room, and the supposed reason she had required a gun in the first place. What if the address book and diary had been made to disappear because they contained incriminating evidence about her private life?

Then there was Arthur Haynes' focus on Audrey's religion. The story told by her defence lawyer, and supported by her mother, was that Audrey had been educated in a convent and was a devout Catholic. According to her testimony, Audrey had sat in church with her rosary, contemplating taking her own life, before deciding to take revenge on Cyril Gidley, who had assaulted her and then broken off their relationship so that he could continue to be a 'lad about town'. This was the evidence presented to the jury. But all was not as it seemed. Hubert Parker later found out that Audrey had allegedly only converted to

11. '... PROBABLE HEART ATTACK'

Catholicism a few days before the trial—a questionable timeframe for conversion in itself. Parker also claimed Haynes challenged protestant jurors so that he could secure a Catholic majority. Neither of these claims can be substantiated further.

The character of the accused needs to be considered. Audrey was a twenty-year-old art student of Anglo descent who was portrayed as coming from a respectable, hardworking family. Her beauty and fashionable clothing were noted in the newspaper stories and the photographs accompanying them. The 'optics' of this would have had an impact on how the public perceived her and how the jury might more sympathetically receive her. Imagine for a moment if she had not come from a background of relative privilege—if she was not white, not 'respectable', and if the killing had not taken place in a society setting. Would the result have been the same? On the other hand, the prosecution could have done much to subvert these biases. Audrey's large family seems to have been more aspirational working class than established middle class. It might have been possible to paint Audrey as a young woman of loose morals given her parents' concerns about her frequenting the docks and the presence of a condom in her handbag.

Another possible missed opportunity in the prosecution's case occurred when Parker did not go into a thorough examination of whether alleged claims Cyril Gidley made against Edward Jacob were in fact true. The object of the defence case was to portray Cyril as calculating, manipulative and mean. He had driven Audrey to act as she had. Her family life was a mess and Cyril had been the root cause of it. But what if Cyril hadn't been? What if Edward Jacob—a man in an upstanding occupation—was acting inappropriately outside of his marriage? Would that have affected the jury's sympathies?

Years before, in January 1906, the Kalgoorlie *Sun* reported that a Boulder clerk of courts, clerk of petty sessions, and district registrar had 'forced his attentions on a young married woman'. The paper confirmed the matter had been subject to a departmental report and was being reported to the public because it concerned an official in 'a fairly high and exceedingly responsible position'. A young married woman (unnamed in the story) had come to him in December 1905 to register her three-and-a-half-month-old baby. The registrar got the relevant paperwork but began 'to initiate a little love-making on his own account'. Afterwards he made an excuse that the paperwork was not correct, so she would have to visit him again. He asked the young woman where she lived and when he bumped into her in the street, he told her: 'I'm coming up to see you tonight.' The woman told her husband who promptly went down to see the registrar at his work. A fight broke out and the husband took the 'Lothario', as the paper labelled him, to the police station. A police officer pointed out the respectable position of the registrar and told the husband he would need to take out a summons. This didn't eventuate and the newspaper speculated that the husband might well have thought black eyes would teach the registrar a lesson. The registrar also did not proceed with reporting the assault.

The registrar was named only as 'Jacob' in the newspaper report. The work description fits Edward Jacob's employment. There's no census record matching Edward Jacob in Kalgoorlie–Boulder at the time, but he could have been working away from Jessie and their young children for a short period, as he was known to do. Or possibly the family was with him, though there is no record for them being there. There is, however, a census entry for 1906 in which Edward and Jessie Jacob are listed as living in Lincoln Street, Perth. Had Edward been sent back to the city following the incident in January? Does this snippet of information mean that Edward Jacob continued to flirt with other women or that he had extramarital affairs after the Boulder incident in 1906? None of this was raised at the inquest and trial. The defence would not have wanted to show that Edward Jacob had prior form with making passes at women. That would have given credence to Cyril's allegations about Audrey's parents' marriage and her father's activities when he had been living out of home in 1924.

Arthur Haynes' careful management of the public telling of the murder story, inquest and trial remains one of the most important factors in considering the outcome of this case. As historian Caroline Ingram has argued in her own research into the murder of Cyril Gidley, Arthur Haynes' 'deliberate manipulation of the press reports meant that these texts had become more than just a means of selling newspapers: they had become a vehicle for influencing the jury's verdict'.

The media sensationalism didn't end with the trial verdict. As Michael Adams has pointed out in his *Forgotten Australians* podcast, there was a great deal of speculation about Audrey's activities in Melbourne, though there's no solid evidence to confirm that she and Roger ever met with Henry Tacke. However, if Audrey's interview with *Truth* newspaper back in Fremantle was in fact correct, then she herself was adding to some of the speculation.

Avid interest aside, Audrey Jacob shot Cyril Gidley dead on the dancefloor of Government House in August 1925. He had died as a result of the revolver going off, from a wound sustained to the heart. Was it an accidental shooting? Arthur Haynes was tasked with defending his client and he was an astute lawyer. He wanted to win a case which would contribute to his legal reputation. But did he want to win it so much that he was willing to falsify evidence?

The police and prosecution thought they had a straightforward case. Hubert Parker underestimated Arthur Haynes' ability to not only cast doubt over key pieces of police evidence but also the strength of his connections with the media. It was a case won in part on the public relations campaign of a lawyer who knew members of the jury might be influenced by what they were learning about Audrey in the newspapers. Hubert Parker had pleaded with the jury to ignore what they had seen in the press but had they really discarded it in their verdict?

Should all of this detract from Audrey having a case against a partner assaulting her and then her lawyer making the unusual claim that the 'unwritten law' be applied? If Cyril had assaulted Audrey, and if she *was* a victim of a sexual assault, then perhaps it was reasonable to proceed with the defence of a young woman being pushed to her limits into a revenge killing.

The Cyril Gidley case continues to fascinate, not least because it is one of the most sensational murder cases Perth has ever seen. It is a case where people continue to have different interpretations, depending largely on how they see the two protagonists in this case.

Was Cyril Gidley a hapless victim or a manipulative rapist, or something in between? Did Audrey Jacob get away with murder? Did she get off 'scot-free'? Was she just a cold-blooded killer or a woman suffering from post-traumatic stress who suddenly, or finally, 'snapped'?

We will never know the exact truth of what happened, but the Cyril Gidley murder case presents historians with an important example of the very real situation we face at times when we are trying to make sense of the past. In this instance, presented with the remaining evidence and key people who are no longer alive to give their testimonies to a researcher, there exists a gap in the historical record. With all the remaining records and the gaps that might exist, historians have to make their own deliberations and interpretations about the evidence from the past.

The police and the prosecution were right: Cyril Gidley was dead and could not defend himself. Had he survived the gunshot wound, he would have been able to throw more light on the accusations being levelled at him by the defence. But we will never have Cyril's side of the story. And Audrey, as far as we know, never talked publicly about the case after 1926.

Audrey Jacob did, however, share her experience of incarceration in a published account for the *Mirror* newspaper on 17 October 1925 in a story titled 'My six weeks in the shadow of the gallows!'. Dramatised, sensationalised, whatever we make of this account, it gives some voice to Audrey's thoughts at the time—or at least what she wanted to make public. And, guided by her lawyer, it would be a piece that would not incriminate her.

How should history recall Audrey Jacob and the murder of Cyril Gidley?

One thing is certain: Audrey Jacob was found not guilty of shooting Cyril Gidley dead on the dancefloor of Government House in August 1925. This young woman, seen by dozens of witnesses, and holding a smoking gun over her dying ex-lover, escaped the gallows. Guilty or not, Audrey was released from custody and given a second chance. She used that opportunity to marry an American businessman and live out her days in the United States.

11. '... PROBABLE HEART ATTACK'

But the mystery of why Audrey Jacob shot her ex-lover remains, and some haunting stories have come out of Government House over the years. One popular story, which governors also like to tell, is that when a foxtrot plays in the ballroom, the rooms go cold and the lights start flashing—and far worse—when 'Follow Yvette' is played.

Appendix A: 'My Six Weeks in the Shadow of the Gallows!'

MY SIX WEEKS IN THE SHADOW OF THE GALLOWS!

Remarkable Human Document—
Of a Remarkable Girl
FROM ARREST TO ACQUITTAL ON WILFUL MURDER CHARGE.

(Written for "The Mirror" by AUDREY CAMPBELL JACOB.)

To dwell for six terrible weeks under an indictment of wilful murder, in the very shadow of the dreadful gallows, is an experience that happily comes to few people in this world.

Even the most hardened criminal is appalled by the mere suggestion of the law's extremest penalty, even the most callous wrongdoer shrinks from the possibility of a Nemesis such as this.

But to a girl only twenty years old—how much more terrible must this environment and its associations have been.

APPENDIX A: 'MY SIX WEEKS IN THE SHADOW OF THE GALLOWS!'

Audrey Jacob walks the streets a free girl today. Whatever be individual opinions of her act a jury of citizens has set her free. There is nothing more to be said.

She is free. But there are memories that follow, and some of these she attempts to relate in the narrative that follows. "The Mirror" offers it without comment, and without revision.

Hereunder Audrey Jacob tells her own story:

"You are arrested on a charge of wilful murder!"

Looking back now I think that my first memory is that of the utter insignificance that seemed to be attached to those terrible words when they were uttered to me.

If you or anyone dear to you were so addressed by an officer of the law with all those terrible formalities of law that have since become so familiar to me, you can imagine the horrified feeling that would immediately spring up in your breast.

In such a condition was my mind at the time with so many emotions fighting for supremacy in a brain ready to burst that this seemed a vague thing to me.

But events gradually brought me back from what I am sure now must have been a form of complete unconsciousness.

Then each day seemed to bring to me some

NEW REALISATION

of the horror of my position.

Have you ever been under chloroform, and felt as you slowly came out of it that each minute that brought more consciousness, brought more sickness and pain?

Well, if you will understand the picture I think that's how I felt, only the pain was of the mental kind.

It is a new and terrible experience to find yourself stared at. That was my first real torture.

Everybody stared at me. When I sat in court at the inquest I felt the eyes on me like one would feel the rays of the sun. I couldn't get away from them. Everywhere I looked there was some new glance. Some of them were of absolute hate and contempt, most of them were only curiosity, and some of them (may God repay them for it!) were pure pity and sympathy.

And from no one did I receive more consideration than from those woman-officials who were appointed to look after me. I have heard that women make harsh gaolers. Never! They were real Christians.

Every day now new incidents of the past six weeks come back to me and it sometimes seems that it will be a long time before new recollections cease to come I wonder will they ever leave me?

Shall I ever forget

THAT AWFUL MINUTE

when the gates of the gaol at Fremantle closed in on me? Shall I ever forget the clanging of bells, the opening and closing of the great gates, the terrible coldness of those grey stone walls, the awful desolation of everything? I see them now. I see them every night. I wake up in my room, and put on the light some time every night, even yet, before I can realise that I am not in my cell again!

Have you ever spent a night in a cell, you womenfolk who read this? I pray that you never will.

I felt a human being until the door of that cell at Fremantle gaol closed behind me for the first time.

After that I felt—well, just a creature, just a thing that the gaol would

NEVER LET GO

One cell is not much different from another. There is just room for a bed and the barest of fittings. There is a slit for a window, that seemed horrible at first, but I learned to love it afterwards, for I could see the sky through it. You don't know just how I learned to love that little bit of sky.

At eight o'clock every night the lights would go out. After that there was no indication of time, except the booming of that great clock outside the gaol.

I have never been stolid, and perhaps I have always had too much imagination. But I never knew imagination could play such tricks as it used to play in the darkness of the night in that cell.

If I kept my eyes open I could see every detail of the past days come before me: if I closed them horrible shapes and terrible visions would come to taunt me. I have since wondered whether the night in those cells used to make me temporarily mad.

In the daytime I used to feel that whatever punishment came to me the supreme penalty of the law would be withheld.

At night I couldn't comfort myself that way. One day during a little conversation I asked a fellow prisoner in what part of the place the gallows room was. She indicated it with her hand. I wished I hadn't asked her, for every night I found myself looking out from the darkness towards

THAT HORRIBLE ROOM

And then all the thoughts that I scorned in the day used to come to me at night.

One twisted little creature whom I met in the exercise yard, told me that the corridors were haunted by Martha Rendall. I laughed at her then.

But I dared not laugh at night.

I don't like to write the things that I thought I saw. They would sound hopelessly exaggerated, and most people would probably laugh at them. But they seemed terribly real then.

My only friend at night was that little bit of sky I could see through the window-slit. I almost grew to worship that sky, for I could always jump out of bed and run to look at it and know when I saw it that at least I was still in a world that was real.

In my cell you could reach out from wall to wall and one of my half-awake fears was that the walls would crush me. Time upon time I woke up finding myself trying with both hands to push them away.

I can honestly say that I was a coward when darkness came, for all kinds of terrors came with it.

When I did sleep it was only in fits and starts. More than once I woke convinced that there was some shapeless horror lying on the floor just beside my bed. I would then have to get up and look at the sky to be reassured.

When it rained the rain would pelt in through the little window under which I slept, and

BEAT UPON MY FACE

Several times it awakened me with the feeling that someone was raining blows on my face.

One night it was colder than usual, and I pulled the blankets up near to my head. A little later I had a terrible nightmare. I could feel a noose around my neck and it was pressing in and smothering me. When I awoke perspiring all over I found that I had worked the blankets up so tightly round my neck in my sleep that they had almost suffocated me. I shuddered!

On another night I dreamed that a tall woman with her face covered by a black veil came and stooped over my bed. When I asked her in my sleep who she was, she said: "I am Martha Rendall. You must come with me!"

You can picture the horror of it, and when I asked someone next day they told me that Martha Rendall was the last woman hanged in Fremantle and that she always wore a black veil!

But I don't want to say any more about those awful nights.

In the day there was loneliness, but none of the terrors.

The lawn and garden are certainly a wonderful solace for those confined in a gaol, and I found them a paradise. When it was not raining I would be out in the garden and the brightness of the sun and the beautiful creepers and flowers gave me confidence back again.

In the last few days of my detention there I was allowed to paint, and that made a world of difference. For painting you need solitude and detachment. Here I could get both. When I am painting I become engrossed and forget everything else.

You can't imagine how quickly the

DAYS WENT BY

when I had my painting material given me.

I soon found myself fall mechanically into the prison routine; I soon learned to obey promptly, when told, and to ask no questions. I did not come into very close contact with the other female prisoners, but I saw something of them at intervals.

Their attitude had a most depressing effect. Many of them are poor cowed creatures, slinking about and seeming to be forever apologising to the wardresses, apologising for nothing. They hardly seemed like women. I tried to think that whatever happened to me, no matter how long I was compelled to remain in this place I would try not to be like these pitiable, broken-spirited creatures.

But who can tell? It is easy to talk now, but these unfortunates with

THE PRISON BRAND

on them body and soul, may have sometime been strong in spirit until the despair ate into their hearts. I can picture it, for at times even though I had not been placed on trial, I felt that I was beginning to despair, to give up hope, to cease to have the will to fight for myself.

It is no more figure of speech to say that the six weeks I spent were in the shadow of something terrible. For that's how it all seemed. That feeling never once left me entirely. Sleeping and waking the shadow seemed to be forever hanging over me.

And now the shadow is gone.

I am a free girl.

From totally unknown people I have received scores of letters and telegrams congratulating me on my release. That's

ONE SIDE OF THE CASE

There is another.

Yesterday as I walked down the street I heard some lady say to another:

"Fancy her getting off scot free!"

I suppose that lady is not alone in her opinion. I suppose that lots of people are saying the same thing.

I don't blame them. No doubt it seems that way. But I want to tell them something.

I have not got off scot free.

The law has given me liberty. But a jury's verdict cannot wipe away memories. And as God is my judge

APPENDIX A: 'MY SIX WEEKS IN THE SHADOW OF THE GALLOWS!'

the memories still pursue me, and I know they will all my life.

And I can never forget the action of a number of sportsmen at Tattersalls Club in raising a very substantial sum of money for my defence prior to a relative of mine undertaking the liability. This was truly an act of Christian charity.

Please, please don't picture me as a girl who is glorifying herself and imagining she is

A SORT OF HEROINE

I want you to believe that I am really not like that. I am not annoyed if anybody should say nasty things about me. I am too proud and thankful to think that so many of my fellow human-beings have sympathised with me, knowing the little they do of the whole position.

Do you think I could feel proud when I have had to confess myself with the whole of the public as my confessor? The only plea I try to offer on behalf of myself, even now, is that I have been very, very weak, and foolish if you like. But I want to make the rest of my life better.

I have been criticised for wanting to stay here where my family are.

Perhaps if folks knew ALL the reasons—reasons too sacred to tell—they would understand better.

During the last few weeks I have learned to know the true value of

REAL RELIGION

At times I have doubted, but things have happened to me of late that make me know that at the back of everything there is this Great Power Who knows all and sees all, and is merciful to all.

Perhaps I will be criticised for writing all this for a public newspaper. But don't take it the wrong way. I am not bidding for publicity or notoriety. God knows, I have had enough of both. But since I have been forced to say so much in public, I felt that I wanted to tell a little more in my own way unhindered by any rules of court procedure and evidence.

That's why I have written this.

As for the future, well—your kind thought and your prayers can help me!

Acknowledgements

This book developed out of general research I was conducting into crime in Western Australia. I came across references to the *Rex v Audrey Jacob* case and was drawn into the archives by the question of Audrey's culpability in the murder of Cyril Gidley. As a historian and writer, I've been interested in crime stories featuring women—on either side of the law—for some years now. The trial of Audrey Jacob provided me with a case still being discussed and debated today.

It was a moment in the State Records Office of Western Australia that really brought the reality of the case home for me. The fabulous staff at the State Records Office tracked down a file I had been looking for but, as it turned out, it was held in the Supreme Court archival collections. It was with great anticipation that Gerard Foley brought the file to me, watching as I opened it and discovering what he also had not expected. There, in the prosecution file, was the empty cartridge from the one round Audrey had fired. It's these finds that really bring the past to life.

This project has been greatly assisted by the support of staff at the State Records Office of Western Australia. The police, court and other files all helped to bring the case to life for me. I know that Damien Hassan had a special interest in this story, and that mattered a great deal. I would like to also thank Gerard Foley, Damien Hassan and

David Whiteford for their continuing enthusiasm in this work and genuine support for researchers. My thanks also to Damian Shepherd, the Director of the State Records Office, for the invitation to deliver the Geoffrey Bolton Lecture in November 2020 and for taking a genuine interest in my research and writing.

I would like to thank my publisher and editor, Georgia Richter, at Fremantle Press. Georgia's support for my projects has been unwavering. Thank you. Georgia and the whole team at Fremantle Press demonstrate what it means to support great Australian stories and ensure every author feels incredibly important and special. Each book that is published by Fremantle Press is done with the highest level of professionalism and a nice dose of excitement. I'm so very proud of what the team has created with my book but even more pleased to be a part of a Fremantle Press community of wonderful and talented people. Someone said to me recently that what they love about Fremantle Press books is each one is exquisitely presented. Yes, they are.

Thank you to Toni Church who worked at the Old Law Court Museum in Perth while I was writing this book. I really appreciate you going through the collection to find archival material which has contributed to the telling of this story.

I would also like to thank three researchers for the support they have offered to the writing of this book. Two or three years ago when I was working on another project and toying with whether or not to pursue the Audrey story further, the notable Australian historian Kay Saunders told me that I absolutely had to write the book and that I was the best person to do so. Professor Saunders is a distinguished writer with her own valuable contributions to what we know about women and crime.

My thanks also to Caroline Ingram who is currently completing a PhD at The University of Western Australia. Caroline and I have crossed paths many times over the years at conferences, talks and in research rooms. Caroline's PhD thesis is on women appearing before the Supreme Court of Western Australia and some of her research has featured Audrey Jacob. Given our similar interests, I'm grateful to Caroline for supporting this book and sharing her own thoughts on the case. I know that your wider research is going to really expand what we know about women before the courts.

Michael Adams, a brilliant author and storyteller, also shares my interest in the Audrey Jacob case and has featured the story in his brilliant *Forgotten Australia* podcast (and forthcoming book developed out of the podcast on forgotten histories). With unwavering generosity, Michael shared some of his research with me, and though we had looked through the same records, Michael pointed me in the direction of more records relating to Audrey's life after she left Australia. Thank you.

I am grateful for the support from my colleagues at The University of Notre Dame Australia. There's been too many moments to list here when a spark of creativity has been lit by a conversation with a colleague and sometimes from someone in a completely unrelated field to my own. Thanks especially to Shane Burke for the great banter we have at work. While I know you will never accept that historians are better than archaeologists, we can at least agree on supporting Swan Districts.

Thanks to Tom Gannon for your humour and support. And dad jokes, I guess. Thanks also to Simon Adams. You had a huge impact on me as an emerging academic and I really value our ongoing connection. My thanks also to the Morgan family. To Maria and Colin and your beautiful family, you really mean the world to me.

To the many university students who have suffered my off-the-topic humour, thank you for respectfully staying with me through a whole course! In my more than two decades of working in universities, perhaps the most important thing I have learned is that I know more because of what *I* have learned from all the different people who have filled lecture theatres and tutorial rooms to learn from me. The learning experience has been a two-way journey. Thank you.

Deepest thanks to friends and family in Australia, Scotland, the United States and many other places around the world who all have a special place in my heart. Special thanks to my mum and dad for being my best pals. Thanks to Debbie Straw for your love and genuine interest in my books. Thanks to Amanda Wright for being, I reckon, the first friend to rush out and buy any of my books.

Thanks also to my great pal, Larry Writer. I was such a fangirl when I first met you in 2016, when you contacted me to congratulate me on my Kate Leigh book, and when I could hardly contain my nervousness in meeting you. Since then, your words of support have always inspired me and your belief in my writing abilities has got me through some patches where I was second-guessing myself. Our shared love of F. Scott Fitzgerald is an added bonus to an already special friendship.

The best thing that has ever happened to me was meeting and marrying my husband, Tony. Through every book I've researched and written, Tony has been there to listen to my ideas, support me when deadlines loom, and love me through the highs and lows of combining writing with full-time work and bringing up our three boys. Tony is still my biggest crush, and even Robert Redford can't compare! Thank you to our boys, Jack, Lawson and Riley, for the cuddles, laughs and love that make each day special. And Evie too! I'm proud to be your dog-mum.

Notes

PROLOGUE: 'FLASH OF FIRE'

Lived experience of Sergeant William Brodie

Back in 1902, when he was a twenty-six-year-old Gippsland bushman still new to the Western Australian Police Force, William Brodie had been in hot pursuit of the notorious horse-stealing bandit, Jack Baker. Given his bush skills, Brodie worked in the mounted branch and it was largely down to him that Baker was trailed from Bulls Creek (now Bullcreek) to Kelmscott, out to Parkerville and Mundaring, and finally to Upper Swan. He located the horse, and Baker himself was later arrested much further north, at Geraldton.

See: 'POLICE CAREER. Experiences of Sergeant W. Brodie', *West Australian*, 4 March 1938, p.14, trove.nla.gov.au/newspaper/article/41664681.

'Perth was more like a large country town …'

The gold rushes from the 1880s had tripled the population of Western Australia from fewer than 50,000 people in 1889 to 170,000 by the close of the century. As the state's capital, Perth's population also increased dramatically from around 6,000 people in 1884 to 27,000 in 1901, then more than tripled to 87,000 by 1911. But this was still a fraction of the populations of larger Australian cities. Sydney's population was already 50,000 in the 1880s and had risen to over a million by 1925, with Melbourne next at over 800,000 people.

See: *Statistical Register of Western Australia,* Part 1 – Population and Vital Statistics, Population, Government Printer, Perth, p.3; T.C. Stannage, *The People of Perth: A Social History of Western Australia's Capital City,* pp.241, 243, 188, 293; 'POPULATION OF SYDNEY', *Barrier Miner* (Broken Hill, NSW), 17 December 1925, p.1, trove.nla.gov.au/newspaper/article/45919765; Michael Pacione, *Urban Geography: A Global Perspective,* pp.142–143.

In the regular business of their day-to-day work, Brodie and other officers mainly dealt with good-order offences such as drunkenness, illegal betting, idle and disorderly, and loitering for prostitution. While Perth didn't have the organised crime problems of the larger cities, Brodie and other officers were already hearing some interesting stuff being passed along policing circles that Sydney was fast becoming the cocaine capital of Australia.

Alfred W. McCoy, *Drug Traffic: Narcotics and Organised Crime in Australia*; Peter N. Grabosky, *Sydney in Ferment: Crime, Dissent and Official Reaction 1788–1973*; Larry Writer, *Razor: Tilly Devine, Kate Leigh and the Razor Gangs.*

Government House

Heritage Council, InHerit, 'Government House and Grounds', heritage report, 2021, inherit.stateheritage.wa.gov.au/Public/Inventory/Details/41687ad7-fb08-45d0-9e16-cb71480eb3f2.

Gladys Moncrieff

Peter Burgis, 'Moncrieff, Gladys Lillian (1892–1976)', *Australian Dictionary of Biography*, National Centre of Biography, Australian National University, adb.anu.edu.au/biography/moncrieff-gladys-lillian-7621/text13319.

The Shooting

SROWA, 'Cyril Gidley – re. Murder of at Perth', AU WA S76, con. 430, 1925/5963; SROWA, 'Supreme Court, Criminal Sittings, Perth 6th October 1925', AU WA A44, con. 3473, item 560, case number 5533;

'BALLROOM TRAGEDY!', *Daily News* (Perth), 27 August 1925, p.10, trove.nla.gov.au/newspaper/article/78442805; SROWA, Detective Sergeant Frazer's report for Inspector Condon, 'Cyril Gidley – re. Murder of at Perth', AU WA S76, con. 430, 1925/5963.

1. FREMANTLE FLAPPER

Audrey Jacob's family background

Ancestry.com. *Victoria, Australia, Assisted and Unassisted Passenger Lists, 1839–1923* [database online]. Provo, UT, USA: Ancestry.com Operations Inc., 2009; Ancestry.com. *Australia, Electoral Rolls, 1903–1980* [database online]. Provo, UT, USA: Ancestry.com Operations, Inc., 2010.

Fremantle

Davidson, *Fremantle Impressions*, pp.78, 122, 234; Patricia M. Brown, *The Merchant Princes of Fremantle: The Rise and Decline of a Colonial Elite 1870–1900*.

'brothel between two churches'

'A Black Blot', *Truth* (Perth), 29 August 1903, p.2, trove.nla.gov.au/newspaper/article/207385696.

South Fremantle for the 'racehorse and battler'

Davidson, *Fremantle Impressions*, p.234.

Fremantle's criminal side

'A Fremantle Robbery', *The West Australian*, 1 January 1903, p.4, trove.nla.gov.au/newspaper/article/24851501; 'News and Notes. Crime and Light', *West Australian*, Friday 4 April 1924, p.10, trove.nla.gov.au/newspaper/article/31224247; 'Persons of Evil Fame', *West Australian*, Tuesday 12 May 1903, p.7, trove.nla.gov.au/newspaper/article/24823553.

Cosmopolitan Fremantle

Davidson, *Fremantle Impressions*, p.126; Reece and Pascoe, *A Place of Consequence*, p.53.

Junner background details (painter)

Ancestry.com. *Victoria, Australia, Assisted and Unassisted Passenger Lists, 1839–1923* [database online]. Provo, UT, USA: Ancestry.com Operations Inc., 2009.

Audrey Jacob's artistic ability

'PAINTED A NUMBER OF PICTURES', *Mirror* (Perth), 5 September 1925, p.2, trove.nla.gov.au/newspaper/article/76445583.

Flappers

Judith Mackrell, *Flappers: Six Women of a Dangerous Generation*, pp.5–11; 'Decadent times', *Northern Star* (Lismore), 7 September 1921, p.2, trove.nla.gov.au/newspaper/article/93106991; Linda Simon, *Lost Girls: The Invention of the Flapper*, pp.8–11; Arthur Mizener, *The Far Side of Paradise: A Biography of F. Scott Fitzgerald*, p.xii; F. Scott Fitzgerald, *The Great Gatsby*; F. Scott Fitzgerald, *The Crack-Up*; Thomas Keneally, *Australians: Flappers to Vietnam*, pp.13–15.

Flappers in Fremantle

'Promenading Flappers', *Advertiser* (Fremantle), 25 January 1924, p.1, trove.nla.gov.au/newspaper/article/255937274.

'... heartrending amongst the local flappers ...'

'FREMANTLE FROLICS', *Mirror* (Perth), 19 May 1923, p.7, trove.nla.gov.au/newspaper/article/77756955.

Background information for Cyril Gidley

There's some conflicting information about Cyril Gidley's age. Ancestry records have him as born in 1901. However, Cyril's death certificate identifies him as twenty-five years of age. His father's name is also incorrectly given as 'Samuel' in newspaper reports about his death and funeral. Cyril's father wrote letters to the police in Perth and signed them as 'Joseph A. Gidley. Father of deceased'.

See: SROWA, 'Cyril Gidley – re. Murder of at Perth'.

NOTES

Audrey's parents', especially her father's, disapproval of relationship
SROWA, 'Supreme Court of Western Australia, Criminal Indictment Register 4'.

2. 'I SEE BLOOD BETWEEN YOU'

'... those who believe in Fate': Audrey and Cyril consult fortune-teller
'"YOU WILL NOT MARRY"', *Mirror* (Perth), 12 September 1925, p. 1, trove.nla.gov.au/newspaper/article/76446071.

Fortune-tellers background
Alana Piper, '"A Menace and an Evil": Fortune-telling in Australia, 1900–1918', *History Australia*, pp.53–73; Alana Piper, 'Women's Work: The Professionalisation and Policing of Fortune-Telling in Australia', pp.37–52; Circular from the Prime Minister's Office, 30 March 1917, Item 318941, Series 16855, Queensland State Archives.

Police Act 1892, section 66
Western Australian Parliament, *Western Australia. Police Act 1892–1967*, section 66, pp.35–37, legislation.wa.gov.au/legislation/prod/filestore.nsf/FileURL/mrdoc_17653.pdf/$FILE/POLICE%20ACT%201892%20-%20%5B03-00-00%5D.pdf?OpenElement.

Catherine Hill charged with false pretences in July 1917
'COME THIS WAY', *Daily News* (Perth), 6 July 1917, p.7, trove.nla.gov.au/newspaper/article/81016284; 'FORTUNE TELLING', *West Australian*, 18 July 1917, p.8, trove.nla.gov.au/newspaper/article/27305495.

'I see blood between you'
'"YOU WILL NOT MARRY"', *Mirror* (Perth), 12 September 1925, p.1, trove.nla.gov.au/newspaper/article/76446071.

Audrey at the ball
Old Court House Law Museum, Audrey Jacob's recalling of events in 'TRIAL NOTES, AUDREY JACOB 1925'.

'Sweet memories'
SROWA, Hermann Conrad Goerling statement to the police, 29 September, 1925 in 'Rex versus Audrey C. Jacob'.

The Shooting
SROWA, 'Cyril Gidley – re. Murder of at Perth'; SROWA, 'Supreme Court, Criminal Sittings, Perth 6th October 1925'; 'BALLROOM TRAGEDY', *Daily News* (Perth), 27 August 1925, p.10, trove.nla.gov.au/newspaper/article/78442805; SROWA, Detective Sergeant Frazer's report for Inspector Condon, 'Cyril Gidley – re. Murder of at Perth'.

3. '... TO KEEP HER OWN COUNSEL'

Detective Sergeant Frazer visiting Audrey in the lock-up
SROWA, 'Supreme Court of Western Australia, Criminal Indictment Register 4'.

Esther Warden
'Port Paragraphs', *Sunday Times*, 27 July 1913, p.15, trove.nla.gov.au/newspaper/article/57808337; '"A PERFECT FIEND"', *Daily News*, 20 January 1914, p.3, trove.nla.gov.au/newspaper/article/80100125; 'PERTH POLICE COURT', *West Australian*, 1 October 1917, p.3, trove.nla.gov.au/newspaper/article/27456027.

DS Frazer mentioned at inquest he was called out to investigation
'"This Note Is In Case She Does Keep Her Vow"', *Truth* (Perth), 12 September 1925, p.5, trove.nla.gov.au/newspaper/article/208127255.

Weather in Perth on 27 August
'LOCAL BUREAU'S REPORT', *West Australian*, 27 August 1925, p.10, trove.nla.gov.au/newspaper/article/31876861/2746921.

NOTES

Press report about the shooting and Audrey's appearance in police court

'SUMMED UP', *Daily News* (Perth), 27 August 1925, p.1, trove.nla.gov.au/newspaper/article/78442739; 'BALLROOM TRAGEDY', *Daily News* (Perth), 27 August 1925, p.10, trove.nla.gov.au/newspaper/article/78442805/7930861.

Audrey appearing 'undisturbed and unemotional'

'SHOT DEAD', *Labor Daily* (Sydney), 28 August 1925, p.1, trove.nla.gov.au/newspaper/article/238124910.

Arthur Haynes' family background

'DEATH OF MR. HAYNES', *West Australian*, 22 February 1922, p.7, trove.nla.gov.au/newspaper/article/28161645; 'Mr. A.G. Haynes, appearing for Walsh and Flynn', *Mirror* (Perth), 27 July 1935, p.15, trove.nla.gov.au/newspaper/article/75716059.

Arthur Haynes visiting Audrey and trying to visit Audrey's parents

Old Court House Law Museum, Arthur Haynes itemising his visits and costs in 'TRIAL NOTES, AUDREY JACOB 1925', 1987.37.

'… to keep her own counsel'

'A Tragic Ending To a Charity Ball', *Truth* (Perth), 29 August 1925, p.1, trove.nla.gov.au/newspaper/article/208127063.

Edward Cutting and William Murphy identify the body

SROWA, 'Cyril Gidley – re. Murder of at Perth', AU WA S76, con. 430, 1925/5963; Ancestry.com. *Australia, Electoral Rolls, 1903–1980* [database online]. Provo, UT, USA: Ancestry.com Operations, Inc., 2010.

Matthew Waddell, orderly who stripped Cyril's body

SROWA, 'Supreme Court of Western Australia, Criminal Indictment Register 4', AU WA A44, con. 3473, item 560, case number 5533.

Donald Stuart MacKenzie background details

Donald's middle name was incorrectly written as 'Stewart' in the inquest and trial records, and thus reported in the press. Donald remarried in 1926 and died aged 72 in 1956. There was more family loss after his first wife's death, however. Family records shared on Ancestry.com reveal Donald's eldest daughter, Rosalind, died in Perth in 1936 aged just twenty-one. His only son, John, passed away when he was forty-seven, leaving behind a wife and three children.

For background information about Donald MacKenzie see: NAA, 'MacKenzie Donald Stuart : SERN MAJOR : POB Goulburn NSW : POE N/A : NOK W MacKenzie Margaret'; 'DEATHS', *West Australian*, 5 June 1925, p.1, trove.nla.gov.au/newspaper/article/31861638; 'Woman's World: PERSONAL', *Western Mail* (Perth), 11 June 1925, p.27, trove.nla.gov.au/newspaper/article/37648906.

Cyril Gidley post-mortem

SROWA, Memo from the Deputy Superintendent, 22 January 1926, 'Cyril Gidley – re. Murder of at Perth'; Donald Stewart MacKenzie deposition in SROWA, 'Supreme Court, Criminal Sittings, Perth 6th October 1925'; Old Court House Law Museum, 'Exhibit D' in 'transcript of exhibits', 1987.37 b-d.

Cyril Gidley article

'BALLROOM TRAGEDY!', *Daily News* (Perth), 27 August 1925, p.10, trove.nla.gov.au/newspaper/article/78442806.

Arthur Haynes and relationship with newspaper editor

Old Court House Law Museum, *Rex v Audrey Campbell Jacob*; Caroline Ingram, 'Constructing Gender in the Press: The Case of Audrey Jacob', pp.58–84.

Victor Courtney background

Ron Davidson, *High Jinks at the Hot Pool*: Mirror *Reflects the Life of a City*, pp.20–27.

NOTES

1924 murder case

Ron Davidson, *High Jinks at the Hot Pool,* pp.62–70.

Mirror article with photographs

'BALLROOM HORROR!', *Mirror* (Perth), 29 August 1925, p.1, trove. nla.gov.au/newspaper/article/76443279.

Cyril Gidley's funeral

'THE LATE MR. CYRIL GIDLEY', *Daily News* (Perth), 2 September 1925, p.8, trove.nla.gov.au/newspaper/article/78445140; 'THE MYSTERIOUS WREATH—HOW IT WAS SENT', *Truth* (Perth), 17 October 1925, p.5, trove.nla.gov.au/newspaper/article/208127900; 'IN MEMORIAM', *West Australian,* 27 August 1926, p.1, trove.nla. gov.au/newspaper/article/31944976.

Edward Cutting, pallbearer

SROWA, 'Cyril Gidley – re. Murder of at Perth'; Ancestry.com, *Australia, Electoral Rolls, 1903–1980* [database online]. Provo, UT, USA: Ancestry.com Operations, Inc., 2010.

4. 'THE REMARKABLE EYES OF AUDREY CAMPBELL JACOB'

Audrey and her parents arriving at the inquest

'THE BALLROOM TRAGEDY', *Daily News* (Perth), 3 September 1925, p.12, trove.nla.gov.au/newspaper/article/78447131; photographs were later published in '"This Note Is In Case She Does Keep Her Vow"', *Truth* (Perth), 12 September 1925, p.5, trove.nla.gov.au/ newspaper/article/208127255.

Alfred Kidson background

Alfred Kidson went into retirement in 1931 and died in Perth on 23 May 1937.

See: 'Even Those He Gaoled Liked A.B. Kidson', *Mirror* (Perth), 29 May 1937, p.16, trove.nla.gov.au/newspaper/article/75456455; Parliament of Western Australia, 'Members' biographical register: Alfred Bowman

Kidson', parliament.wa.gov.au/parliament/library/MPHistoricalData.
nsf/(Lookup)/47D5CF2A511239CA482577E50028A697?).

Edward and Jessie Jacob's depositions at the inquest

SROWA, 'Supreme Court of Western Australia, Criminal Indictment Register 4'; '"This Note Is In Case She Does Keep Her Vow."', *Truth* (Perth), 12 September 1925, p.5, trove.nla.gov.au/newspaper/article/208127255; 'THE BALLROOM TRAGEDY', *Daily News* (Perth), 3 September 1925, trove.nla.gov.au/newspaper/article/78447131, p.12.

Audrey's engagement to Cyril

SROWA, 'Supreme Court of Western Australia, Criminal Indictment Register 4'; 'SOCIAL', *West Australian*, 8 October 1924, p.5, trove.nla.gov.au/newspaper/article/31257155.

Police raids on *Kangaroo*

Jessie Jacob's statement about Cyril Gidley smuggling goods onto the ship he was working on is confirmed by a newspaper report at the time, though Gidley is not mentioned and only the smuggled goods are detailed.

See: 'NEWS AND NOTES. Smuggling on M.S. Kangaroo', *West Australian*, 6 October 1924, p.8, trove.nla.gov.au/newspaper/article/31256684.

Cyril's threatening letters

'INQUEST OPENS', *Mirror* (Perth), 5 September 1925, p.1, trove.nla.gov.au/newspaper/page/7435411.

Police prosecution concerns about defence's portrayal of Cyril Gidley

SROWA, Detective Sergeant Frazer's report for Inspector Condon, 'Cyril Gidley – re. Murder of at Perth'.

Mirror reporting of parents' evidence

'INQUEST OPENS', *Mirror* (Perth), 5 September 1925, p.1, trove.nla.gov.au/newspaper/article/76445571.

Audrey's eyes

'THE REMARKABLE EYES OF AUDREY CAMPBELL JACOB', *Mirror* (Perth), 5 September 1925, p.2, trove.nla.gov.au/newspaper/article/76445587.

5. 'SHE APPEARED TO BE IN A DAZED CONDITION'

Witness depositions 7 and 8 September 1925

SROWA, 'Supreme Court of Western Australia, Criminal Indictment Register 4'.

Arthur Haynes cross-examining witnesses on 7 September

'BALLROOM TRAGEDY', *West Australian*, 8 September 1925, p.7, trove.nla.gov.au/newspaper/article/31879037.

Background information for Alfred Timms

'Mentioned in Dispatches', *Sunday Times* (Perth), 25 February 1934, p.10, trove.nla.gov.au/newspaper/article/58715094; 'SINGING POLICE INSPECTOR RETIRES', 13 November 1943, p.10, trove.nla.gov.au/newspaper/article/78399313.

Annie Humphreys photograph and testimony

SROWA, 'Supreme Court of Western Australia, Criminal Indictment Register 4'; '"This Note Is In Case She Does Keep Her Vow."', *Truth* (Perth), 12 September 1925, p.5, trove.nla.gov.au/newspaper/article/208127255.

William Murphy and Violet Murphy testimony

'BALLROOM TRAGEDY', *West Australian*, 8 September 1925, p.8, trove.nla.gov.au/newspaper/article/31879037/2752181; '"This Note Is In Case She Does Keep Her Vow."', *Truth* (Perth), 12 September 1925, p.5, trove.nla.gov.au/newspaper/article/208127255; 'A Prophetic

Letter', *Truth* (Perth), 12 September 1925, p.5, trove.nla.gov.au/newspaper/article/208127253/22664700.

Cyril Gidley's letter

SROWA, Cyril Gidley signed letter, 16 August 1925 in 'Rex versus Audrey C. Jacob'. Details about the letter were also published in: '"This Note Is In Case She Does Keep Her Vow"', *Truth* (Perth), 12 September 1925, p.5, trove.nla.gov.au/newspaper/article/208127255, where the single word on the front of Cyril's envelope was recorded as 'The' rather than 'She'.

Russell Sandeman and Frederick Crowder testimony

'"This Note Is In Case She Does Keep Her Vow"', *Truth* (Perth), 12 September 1925, p.5, trove.nla.gov.au/newspaper/article/208127255.

Maude Mitchell fainting after the shooting

'DRAMATIC DANCE OF DEATH', *Sunday Times* (Perth), 30 August 1925, p.1, trove.nla.gov.au/newspaper/article/58226800.

Maude Mitchell's responses as reported in the press

'BALLROOM TRAGEDY', *West Australian*, 9 September 1925, p.10, trove.nla.gov.au/newspaper/article/31879098.

Cross-examination of Mitchell, Frazer and Courtney

'BALLROOM TRAGEDY', *West Australian*, 9 September 1925, p.10, trove.nla.gov.au/newspaper/article/31879098.

Witness depositions, 14 September 1925

SROWA, 'Supreme Court of Western Australia, Criminal Indictment Register 4'. The order of the witnesses in the inquest was also matched against the police records; '"This Note Is In Case She Does Keep Her Vow"', *Truth* (Perth), 12 September 1925, p.5, trove.nla.gov.au/newspaper/article/208127255; 'CHARGE OF WILFUL MURDER', *Mirror* (Perth), 19 September 1925, p.10, trove.nla.gov.au/newspaper/article/76442916.

Arthur Haynes unhappy with inquest proceedings towards a finding
'CHARGE OF WILFUL MURDER', *Mirror* (Perth), 19 September 1925, p.10, trove.nla.gov.au/newspaper/article/76442916.

Coroner Kidson's ruling
SROWA, 'Supreme Court of Western Australia, Criminal Indictment Register 4'.

Mirror newspaper reporting the decision
'CHARGE OF WILFUL MURDER', *Mirror* (Perth), 19 September 1925, p.10, trove.nla.gov.au/newspaper/article/76442916.

Martha Rendell hanging
'Execution of Martha Rendell', *Westralian Worker*, 8 October 1909, p.4, trove.nla.gov.au/newspaper/article/148597023; Anna Haebich, 'Murdering Stepmothers: The trial and execution of Martha Rendell', *Journal of Australian Studies,* vol. 22 (1998), pp.66–81.

6. '... TO BLACKEN THE CHARACTER OF THE DECEASED'

Inspector Condon
SROWA, Police Department Western Australia, 'Personal file – Condon, S (regimental file no. 38).

DS Frazer's police report for the Crown Prosecutor
SROWA, 'Cyril Gidley – re. Murder of at Perth'.

Assault of a girl in 1916
'Tale of a Tent.', *Truth* (Perth), 19 August 1916, p.5, trove.nla.gov.au/newspaper/article/211810660; 'RETURNED SOLDIER'S CRIME'. *Kalgoorlie Miner,* 7 September 1916, p.5, trove.nla.gov.au/newspaper/article/92162212.

Robert Connell, Commissioner of Police
Robert Connell was the Commissioner of Police from 1913–1933 and was determined to turn the Western Australian Police Force into a

more professional outfit. He oversaw the introduction of fingerprint technology which would revolutionise criminal investigations. He was moved by the social issues of the day and worked hard to campaign the state government to properly address problems such as gambling, child abuse, deserted wives and prostitution. Commissioner Connell also supported the introduction of women into policing in Western Australia.

See: SROWA, Police Department Western Australia, 'Robert Connell – Commissioner of Police Personal file', con. 1496, 1933/0164.

Hubert Parker's letter to Arthur Haynes

SROWA, Hubert Parker letter, 21 September 1925 in 'Rex versus Audrey C. Jacob'.

Hubert Parker

'NEW CROWN PROSECUTOR', *Kalgoorlie Miner*, 24 December 1920, p.5, trove.nla.gov.au/newspaper/article/92882175; Parliament of Western Australia, 'Hubert Stanley Wyborn Parker', parliament.wa.gov.au/parliament/library/MPHistoricalData.nsf/(Lookup)/17E7B8F9C01843A1482577E50028A75A?OpenDocument.

Edward and Jessie Jacob's meeting with Laura Chipper

SROWA, Laura Chipper's statement for the police prosecution in 'Rex versus Audrey C. Jacob'.

The Women Police background

'Women Police', *Freeman's Journal (NSW)*, 10 June 1915, p. 22, trove.nla.gov.au/newspaper/article/115310057; 'Policewomen Appointed', *Sun* (Sydney), 24 June 1915, p.7, trove.nla.gov.au/newspaper/article/229320145; 'The Feminine Touch', *Daily Herald (Adelaide)*, 28 June 1915, p.3, trove.nla.gov.au/newspaper/article/134416917; 'The Duties Of Policewomen', *Albury Banner and Wodonga Express*, 2 July 1915, p.32, trove.nla.gov.au/newspaper/article/108151277; 'Women Police', *Armidale Chronicle* (NSW), 7 July 1915, p.8, trove.nla.gov.au/newspaper/article/187704820; Hazel King, 'Armfield, Lillian May (1884–1971)', *Australian Dictionary of Biography*, Australian National

University, adb.anu.edu.au/biography/armfield-lillian-may-5050;
'Let's Talk of Interesting People', *Australian Women's Weekly*,
17 November 1934, p.3, trove.nla.gov.au/newspaper/article/48083783;
Leigh Straw, *Lillian Armfield: How Australia's First Female Detective Took on Tilly Devine and the Razor Gangs and Changed the Face of the Force*.

Chipper and Dugdale

Leonie Stella, 'Policing Women: Women's Police in Western Australia 1917–1943', Honours thesis, Murdoch University, 1990, pp.7, 22, 24, 30, 40–42, 50, 58, 68, 69, 120–122, 244–246, 151–252.

Duties of the Women Police

Police Commissioner's Annual Report reported in 'Women Police', *West Australian*, 3 December 1917, p.3, trove.nla.gov.au/newspaper/article/27462229.

Constable Dugdale's 1921 report

Stella, 'Policing Women: Women's Police in Western Australia 1917–1943', pp.252–252.

Statement from Hermann Conrad Goerling

SROWA, Hermann Conrad Goerling statement to the police, 29 September 1925 in 'Rex versus Audrey C. Jacob'.

The return of the *Kangaroo*

'His Mates Knew Nothing of Cyril Gidley's Tragic End Until the Kangaroo Returned to W.A.' *Truth* (Perth), 3 October 1925, p.7, trove.nla.gov.au/newspaper/article/208127615.

7. 'IT IS A DELIBERATE CASE OF WILFUL MURDER': THE TRIAL BEGINS

Audrey in Fremantle Prison

Audrey Jacob's experiences in Fremantle Prison are in large part taken from Audrey's piece written for the *Mirror* newspaper: 'MY SIX

WEEKS IN THE SHADOW OF THE GALLOWS!', *Mirror* (Perth), 17 October 1925, pp.6, 7, trove.nla.gov.au/newspaper/article/76446716.

Audrey's version of events
Old Court House Law Museum, 'TRIAL NOTES, AUDREY JACOB 1925', 1987.37 dk-dx.

Fremantle Prison background
Fremantle Prison, 'The Convict Era', fremantleprison.com.au/history-heritage/history/the-convict-era.

Junner family paying legal expenses
Old Court House Law Museum, Junner cables in 'TRIAL NOTES, AUDREY JACOB 1925'.

Opening of the trial
'THE BALLROOM TRAGEDY', *Daily News* (Perth), 8 October 1925, p.7, trove.nla.gov.au/newspaper/article/84181202; 'THE BALLROOM TRAGEDY', *Geraldton Express*, 9 October 1925, p.5, trove.nla.gov.au/newspaper/article/259268781; 'AUDREY JACOB NOT GUILTY!', *Mirror* (Perth), 10 October 1925, p.1, trove.nla.gov.au/newspaper/article/76444791.

'First case I wish for female jury'
Old Court House Law Museum, Arthur Haynes' notes in 'TRIAL NOTES, AUDREY JACOB 1925'.

Parker's trial notes
I have used Hubert Parker's opening address notes from the Prosecution file to set out his first address to the jury. Parker incorrectly spelled Annie Humphreys' name as 'Humphrey' in his notes but I have corrected this in the text because, when he appeared in court, as per other records, he used the correct name.

See: SROWA, 'Rex versus Audrey C. Jacob'.

The trial

Cyril Gidley – re. Murder of at Perth'; SROWA, 'Supreme Court, Criminal Sittings, Perth 6th October 1925'; SROWA, 'Rex versus Audrey C. Jacob'; Old Court House Law Museum, 'TRIAL NOTES, AUDREY JACOB 1925'; Old Court House Law Museum, Arthur Haynes' notes in 'TRIAL NOTES, AUDREY JACOB 1925'; 'THE BALLROOM TRAGEDY', *Daily News* (Perth), 8 October 1925, p.7, trove.nla.gov.au/newspaper/article/84181202; 'THE BALLROOM TRAGEDY', *Geraldton Express,* 9 October 1925, p.5, trove.nla.gov.au/newspaper/article/259268781.

8. '... THINGS ARE NOT ALWAYS WHAT THEY MAY SEEM': THE TRIAL CONTINUES

The trial continues with Haynes' defence

Cyril Gidley – re. Murder of at Perth'; SROWA, 'Supreme Court, Criminal Sittings, Perth 6th October 1925'; SROWA, 'Rex versus Audrey C. Jacob'; Old Court House Law Museum, 'TRIAL NOTES, AUDREY JACOB 1925'; Old Court House Law Museum, Arthur Haynes' notes in 'TRIAL NOTES, AUDREY JACOB 1925'; 'THE BALLROOM TRAGEDY', *Daily News* (Perth), 8 October 1925, p.7, trove.nla.gov.au/newspaper/article/84181202; 'THE BALLROOM TRAGEDY', *Geraldton Express,* 9 October 1925, p.5, trove.nla.gov.au/newspaper/article/259268781; 'AUDREY JACOB NOT GUILTY!', *Mirror* (Perth), 10 October 1925, p.1, trove.nla.gov.au/newspaper/article/76444791; 'BALLROOM TRAGEDY', *West Australian,* 10 October 1925, p.14, trove.nla.gov.au/newspaper/article/31885202; '"NOT GUILTY"', *Daily Mail* (Brisbane), 10 October 1925, p.6, trove.nla.gov.au/newspaper/article/220638939.

Haynes and evidence against Cyril Gidley

'BALLROOM TRAGEDY', *West Australian,* 9 October 1925, p.13, trove.nla.gov.au/newspaper/article/31884780; 'AUDREY JACOB NOT GUILTY!', *Mirror* (Perth), 10 October 1925, p.1, trove.nla.gov.au/newspaper/article/76444791.

'You may ask did she cry out ...'

'THE BALLROOM TRAGEDY', *Daily News* (Perth), 8 October 1925, p.7, trove.nla.gov.au/newspaper/article/84181202.

Audrey Jacob's testimony

The Old Law Court Museum archives include fifteen pages detailing Audrey's version of events. Previously thought to have been her own written account, they are in fact in the handwriting of her lawyer, Arthur Haynes, as judged by his list of witnesses included in the same file. Audrey's testimony at the trial is also in these archives.

See: Old Court House Law Museum, 'TRIAL NOTES, AUDREY JACOB 1925'.

9. 'IN THE SHADOW OF THE GALLOWS': THE VERDICT

End of the trial

Old Court House Law Museum, 'TRIAL NOTES, AUDREY JACOB 1925'.

Policewoman Dugdale

'BALLROOM TRAGEDY', *West Australian,* 10 October 1925, p.14, trove.nla.gov.au/newspaper/article/31885202.

Testimony of final witnesses

'BALLROOM TRAGEDY', *West Australian,* 10 October 1925, p.14, trove.nla.gov.au/newspaper/article/31885202; 'AUDREY JACOB NOT GUILTY!', *Mirror* (Perth), 10 October 1925, p.1, trove.nla.gov.au/newspaper/article/76444791; 'REMARKABLE SCENES', *Mirror* (Perth), 10 October 1925, p.3, trove.nla.gov.au/newspaper/article/76444784.

The unwritten law

'"NOT GUILTY"', *Daily Mail* (Brisbane), 10 October 1925, p.6, trove.nla.gov.au/newspaper/article/220638939; Caroline Ingram, 'Constructing Gender in the Press: The Case of Audrey Jacob', pp.80–81.

Closing addresses and judge's advice

'AUDREY JACOB NOT GUILTY!', *Mirror* (Perth), 10 October 1925, p.1, trove.nla.gov.au/newspaper/article/76444791; 'REMARKABLE SCENES', *Mirror* (Perth), 10 October 1925, p.3, trove.nla.gov.au/newspaper/article/76444784.

The Verdict

'AUDREY JACOB NOT GUILTY!', *Mirror* (Perth), 10 October 1925, p.1, trove.nla.gov.au/newspaper/article/76444791; 'REMARKABLE SCENES', *Mirror* (Perth), 10 October 1925, p.3, trove.nla.gov.au/newspaper/article/76444784; 'TRIAL OF AUDREY JACOB', *Geraldton Guardian*, 10 October 1925, p.2, trove.nla.gov.au/newspaper/article/67094954.

Audrey's interview with the *Mirror* editor

'AUDREY JACOB INTERVIEWED', *Mirror* (Perth), 10 October 1925, p.3, trove.nla.gov.au/newspaper/article/76444782.

Letter in support of Audrey and collecting money for her studio

'AFTER THE VERDICT', *Mirror* (Perth), 10 October 1925, p.3, trove.nla.gov.au/newspaper/article/76444788.

Letters to the police and Cyril's personal effects itemised

SROWA, 'Rex versus Audrey C. Jacob'.

10. 'I TOLD HIM EVERYTHING'

Jack De Garis

Janet McCalman, 'De Garis, Clement John (Jack) (1884–1926)', *Australian Dictionary of Biography*, National Centre of Biography, Australian National University, adb.anu.edu.au/biography/de-garis-clement-john-jack-5941/text10129, published first in hardcopy 1981, accessed online 20 May 2021; 'VICTORIES OF FAILURE', *News* (Adelaide), 6 June 1925, p.4, trove.nla.gov.au/newspaper/article/129729473; 'WHAT'S THE STRENGTH OF CJ's OIL FIND?',

Truth (Perth), 22 May 1926, p.5, trove.nla.gov.au/newspaper/article/208131963.

Jack De Garis did take his own life. He gassed himself in his Mornington home in August 1926. He was forty-one.

Audrey meets and marries Roger Sinclair

'Audrey Herself Tells Her Story to "Truth" Readers from the Washtub, At Her Mother's Home', *Truth* (Perth), 30 January 1926, p.5, trove.nla.gov.au/newspaper/article/208129962; 'AUDREY JACOB MARRIED!', *Mirror*, 23 January 1926, page 2, trove.nla.gov.au/newspaper/article/76445846.

Audrey Jacob Married

Births, Deaths and Marriages Victoria, 'Jacob, Audrey Campbell'; National Archives and Records Administration; Washington, DC; *Marriage Reports in State Department Decimal Files, 1910–1949*.

Audrey's pearl necklace

'AUDREY JACOB MARRIED!', *Mirror*, 23 January 1926, page 2, trove.nla.gov.au/newspaper/article/76445846.

Henry Tacke murder case

'"Truth" Lifts The Veil from Audrey Jacob, Woman of Mystery', *Truth* (Perth), 30 January 1926, p.5, trove.nla.gov.au/newspaper/article/208129960; trove.nla.gov.au/newspaper/article/208129963.

Audrey back in Fremantle

'Audrey Herself Tells Her Story to "Truth" Readers from the Washtub, At Her Mother's Home', *Truth* (Perth), 30 January 1926, p.5, trove.nla.gov.au/newspaper/article/208129962.

Audrey's relationship with a young Melburnian man

'A CATCH IN IT SOMEWHERE', *Truth* (Perth), 30 January 1926, p.5, trove.nla.gov.au/newspaper/article/208129964.

Audrey Sinclair leaving Fremantle and stranded in Africa story

'An Audrey Jacob Canard THAT IS EASILY EXPLODED', *Mirror* (Perth), 3 July 1926, p.8, trove.nla.gov.au/newspaper/article/76453201.

Cyril Gidley Family Notice

'IN MEMORIUM', *West Australian*, 27 August 1926, p.1, trove.nla.gov.au/newspaper/article/31944976.

Deaths of Edward and Jessie Jacob

'DEATHS', *West Australian*, 28 September 1928, p.1, trove.nla.gov.au/newspaper/article/32226137; 'DEATHS', *West Australian*, 29 April 1929, p.1, trove.nla.gov.au/newspaper/article/32276277.

Hubert Parker

Wendy Birman and G.C. Bolton, 'Parker, Hubert Stanley Wyborn (1883–1966)', *Australian Dictionary of Biography*; 'NEW MEMBERS' CAREERS', *West Australian*, 14 April 1930, p.15, trove.nla.gov.au/newspaper/article/31074117.

Joseph Frazer

'INSPR. FRAZER'S DEATH', *Daily News* (Perth), 14 June 1933, p.5, trove.nla.gov.au/newspaper/article/83225452; 'THE LATE INSPECTOR FRAZER.', *West Australian*, 16 June 1933, trove.nla.gov.au/newspaper/article/32462144.

William Brodie

'POLICE CAREER. Experiences of Sergeant W. Brodie', *West Australian*, 4 March 1938, p.14, trove.nla.gov.au/newspaper/article/41664681.

Alfred Timms

'Mentioned in Despatches', *Sunday Times*, 25 February 1934, p.10, trove.nla.gov.au/newspaper/article/58715094; 'SINGING POLICE INSPECTOR RETIRES', 13 November 1943, p.10, trove.nla.gov.au/newspaper/article/78399313.

Arthur Haynes

'ARTHUR HAYNES CHARGED', *Kalgoorlie Miner*, 5 September 1931, p.4, trove.nla.gov.au/newspaper/article/94952639; 'CHEERED!', *Mirror* (Perth), 19 September 1931, p.6, trove.nla.gov.au/newspaper/article/75766035; 'BRILLIANT BARRISTER PASSES', *Sunday Times* (Perth), 21 September 1952, p.22, trove.nla.gov.au/newspaper/article/60098931; 'A GREAT PERTH LAWYER'S GREATEST CASE', *Mirror* (Perth), 27 September 1952, pp.6, 7, trove.nla.gov.au/newspaper/article/75778684.

Harry Mann

'INSPECTOR HARRY MANN', *Daily News* (Perth), 20 April 1917, p.2, trove.nla.gov.au/newspaper/article/81033688; 'Mr. Harry Mann's Death In Hospital', *Sunday Times* (Perth), 5 October 1952, p, 3, trove.nla.gov.au/newspaper/article/60099541.

Death of Victor Courtney

G.C. Bolton, 'Courtney, Victor Desmond (1894–1970)', *Australian Dictionary of Biography*, National Centre of Biography, Australian National University, adb.anu.edu.au/biography/courtney-victor-desmond-9841/text17407.

11. '... PROBABLE HEART ATTACK'

Vivienne Sinclair

Michael Adams pieced together Audrey's later life from family records and archives available through Ancestry.com. Among other achievements, Vivienne Sinclair worked for the Pentagon in the 1970s and reached the ranking of lieutenant-colonel. It was a remarkable achievement for a woman at the time. Michael kindly shared these records with me, but the credit for the information about Audrey's later life must go to Michael and his telling of this in Michael Adams, 'Murder on the Dancefloor – Part Two'.

Audrey Sinclair's death and grave

Texas Department of Health, Audrey Sinclair's death certificate, State File No. 90382. (The key identifiers on the death certificate correspond with Audrey Sinclair, including the names of her parents and her date and place of birth.); Find a Grave, database and images, findagrave.com/memorial/90545088/audrey-campbell-sinclair, memorial page for Audrey Campbell Jacob Sinclair (9 Feb 1905 – 5 Nov 197).

'Unwritten law' in Australia

Carolyn Ramsay, 'Domestic Violence and State Intervention in the American West and Australia, 1860–1930', p.249; Caroline Ingram, 'Constructing Gender in the Press: The Case of Audrey Jacob', p.80.

Audrey's Catholicism challenged

Hubert Parker's claims were published in a later newspaper article about the ballroom shooting. See James Henderson, 'After 13, The Dance of Death', *Daily News* (Perth), 28 June 1965, pp.14–15.

Edward Jacob, 1906 case

'A BOULDER SCANDAL', *Sun* (Kalgoorlie), 28 January 1906, p.9, trove.nla.gov.au/newspaper/article/211738800.

Ingram on Haynes

Caroline Ingram, 'Constructing Gender in the Press: The Case of Audrey Jacob', p.84.

Michael Adams on the press interest in Audrey

Michael Adams, 'Murder on the Dancefloor – Part Two'.

Audrey Jacob on her time in Fremantle Prison

'MY SIX WEEKS IN THE SHADOW OF THE GALLOWS!', *Mirror* (Perth), 17 October 1925, pp.6, 7, trove.nla.gov.au/newspaper/article/76446716.

References

PRIMARY SOURCES

Births, Deaths, Marriages

Births, Deaths and Marriages Victoria, 'Jacob, Audrey Campbell', 2937/1926, reproduced marriage certificate in possession of the author.

National Archives Australia, Canberra

MacKenzie Donald Stuart : SERN MAJOR : POB Goulburn NSW : POE N/A : NOK W MacKenzie Margaret', in First Australian Imperial Force Personnel Dossiers, 1914–1920, B2455, MACKENZIE D S item 1963095, recordsearch.naa.gov.au/SearchNRetrieve/Interface/DetailsReports/ItemDetail.aspx?Barcode=1963095&isAv=N.

Newspapers

Advertiser (Fremantle)

Albury Banner and Wodonga Express

Armidale Chronicle (NSW)

Australian Women's Weekly

Barrier Miner (Broken Hill)

REFERENCES

Courier Mail (Brisbane)

Daily Mail (Brisbane)

Daily Herald (Adelaide)

Daily News (Perth)

Freeman's Journal (NSW)

Geraldton Express (WA)

Geraldton Guardian (WA)

Goomalling–Dowerin Mail (WA)

Kalgoorlie Miner (WA)

Labor Daily (NSW)

Mirror (Perth)

News (Adelaide)

Northern Star (Lismore NSW)

Sun (Kalgoorlie)

Sun (Sydney)

Sunday Times (Perth)

Truth (Perth)

West Australian (Perth)

Western Mail (Perth)

Old Court House Law Museum, Perth

'Exhibit D' in 'transcript of exhibits', 1987.37 b-d.

Rex v Audrey Campbell Jacob, 1987.37.

'TRIAL NOTES, AUDREY JACOB 1925', 1987.37 dk-dx.

Queensland State Archives

Circular from the Prime Minister's Office, 30 March 1917, Item 318941, Series 16855.

State Library of Western Australia

Government Statistician's Office, *Statistical Register of Western Australia*, 1903–1939, Government Printer, Perth.

State Records Office of Western Australia

'Cyril Gidley – re. Murder of at Perth', AU WA S76, con. 430, 1925/5963.

Police Department Western Australia, 'Robert Connell – Commissioner of Police Personal file', con. 1496, 1933/0164.

Police Department Western Australia, 'Personal file – Condon, S (regimental file no. 38), con. 1065.

'Rex versus Audrey C. Jacob', Crown Law Department, AU WA A68, Item 1925/03517.

Supreme Court, Criminal Sittings, Perth 6th October 1925', AU WA A44, con. 3473, item 560, case number 5533.

Supreme Court, Criminal Indictment Register 4, AU WA A44, con. 3473, item 560, case number 5533.

SECONDARY SOURCES AND FURTHER READING

Allen, Judith A, *Sex and Secrets: Crimes Involving Australian Women since 1880*, Oxford University Press, Melbourne, 1990.

Anleu, Sharyn L. Roach, *Deviance, Conformity & Control*, Pearson, Frenchs Forest, 2006.

Auerbach, Nina, 'The Rise of the Fallen Woman', *Nineteenth-Century Fiction*, vol. 35, no. 1 (June, 1980), pp.29–52.

Bellanta, Melissa, *Larrikins: A History*, University of Queensland Press, St, Lucia, 2012.

Bellanta, Melissa, "The Larrikin Girl", *Journal of Australian Studies: 'the Girl in Australian History'* vol. 34, no. 4 (2010), pp.499–512.

Blaikie, George, *Wild Women of Sydney*, Rigby, Adelaide, 1980.

Bolton, Geoffrey, *Land of Vision and Mirage: Western Australia since 1826*, UWA Press, Crawley, 2008.

REFERENCES

Brown, Patricia M., *The Merchant Princes of Fremantle: The Rise and Decline of a Colonial Elite 1870–1900*, University of Western Australia Press, Nedlands, 1996.

D'Cruze, Shani and Louise A. Jackson (eds), *Women, Crime and Justice in England Since 1660*, Palgrave Macmillan, Hampshire, 2009.

Davidson, Ron, *Fremantle Impressions*, Fremantle Arts Centre Press, Fremantle, 2007.

Davidson, Ron, *High Jinks at the Hot Pool:* Mirror *Reflects the Life of a City*, Fremantle Arts Centre Press, Fremantle, 1994.

Fitzgerald, F. Scott, *The Crack-Up*, James Laughlin, New York, 1945.

Fitzgerald, F. Scott, *The Great Gatsby*, Charles Scribner's Sons, New York, 1925.

Grabosky, Peter N, *Sydney in Ferment: Crime, Dissent and Official Reaction, 1788–1973*, Australian National University Press, Canberra, 1976.

Gregory, Jenny (ed.) *Western Australia Between the Wars 1919–1939: Studies in Western Australian History*, (11) June 1990.

Haebich, Anna, 'Murdering Stepmothers: The trial and execution of Martha Rendell', *Journal of Australian Studies*, vol. 22 (1998), pp.66–81.

Ingram, Caroline, 'Constructing Gender in the Press: The Case of Audrey Jacob', *Law & History*, vol. 6, no. 1 (2019), pp.58–84.

Keneally, Thomas, *Australians (Volume 3): Flappers to Vietnam*, Allen & Unwin, Sydney, 2015.

Mackrell, Judith, *Flappers: Six Women of a Dangerous Generation*, Pan Macmillan, London, 2014.

McCalman, Janet, 'De Garis, Clement John (Jack) (1884–1926)', *Australian Dictionary of Biography*, National Centre of Biography, Australian National University, https://adb.anu.edu.au/biography/de-garis-clement-john-jack-5941/text10129, published first in hardcopy 1981, accessed online 20 May 2021.

McCoy, Alfred W, *Drug Traffic: Narcotics and Organised Crime in Australia*, Harper & Row, Sydney, 1980.

Mizener, Arthur, *The Far Side of Paradise: A Biography of F. Scott Fitzgerald*, Houghton Mifflin, Boston, 1951 (first published 1949).

Pacione, Michael, *Urban Geography: A Global Perspective*, Routledge, New York, 2005.

Piper, Alana, '"A Menace and an Evil": Fortune-telling in Australia, 1900–1918', *History Australia*, vol. 11, no. 3 (2014), pp.53–73.

Piper, Alana, 'Women's Work: The Professionalisation and Policing of Fortune-Telling in Australia', *Labour History*, no. 108 (May 2015), pp.1–16.

Ramsay, Carolyn 'Domestic Violence and State Intervention in the American West and Australia, 1860–1930', *Indiana Law Journal*, 86(1) (2011), p.249, repository.law.indiana.edu/ilj/vol86/iss1/4.

Reece, R. and Pascoe, R., *A Place of Consequence: A Pictorial History of Fremantle*, Fremantle Arts Centre Press, 1983.

Simon, Linda, *Lost Girls: The Invention of the Flapper*, Reaktion Books, London, 2017.

Stannage, T.C., *The People of Perth: A Social History of Western Australia's Capital City*, Carroll's for Perth City Council, Perth, 1979.

Stella, Leonie, 'Policing Women: Women's Police in Western Australia 1917–1943', Honours thesis, Murdoch University, 1990.

Straw, Leigh, *Drunks, Pests and Harlots: Criminal Women in Perth and Fremantle, 1900–1939*, Humming Earth, Kilkerran, 2013.

Straw, Leigh, *Lillian Armfield: How Australia's First Female Detective Took on Tilly Devine and the Razor Gangs and Changed the Face of the Force*, Hachette Australia, 2018.

Writer, Larry, *Razor: Tilly Devine, Kate Leigh and the Razor Gangs*, Pan Macmillan, Sydney, 2009 edition.

REFERENCES

ONLINE RESOURCES

Adams, Michael, 'Murder on the Dancefloor – Part One', *Forgotten Australians*, Podcast, 29 June 2019, forgottenaustralia.com/2019/06/29/murder-on-the-dance-floor-part-one.

Adams, Michael, 'Murder on the Dancefloor – Part Two', *Forgotten Australians*, Podcast, 7 July 2019, forgottenaustralia.com/2019/07/07/murder-on-the-dance-floor-part-two.

Ancestry.com. *Victoria, Australia, Assisted and Unassisted Passenger Lists, 1839–1923* [database online]. Provo, UT, USA: Ancestry.com Operations Inc., 2009.

Ancestry.com. *Australia, Electoral Rolls, 1903–1980* [database online]. Provo, UT, USA: Ancestry.com Operations, Inc., 2010.

Birman, Wendy and G.C. Bolton, 'Parker, Hubert Stanley Wyborn (1883–1966)', *Australian Dictionary of Biography*, National Centre of Biography, Australian National University, adb.anu.edu.au/biography/parker-hubert-stanley-wyborn-8537/text13853, published first in hardcopy 1988, accessed online.

Burgis, Peter, 'Moncrieff, Gladys Lillian (1892–1976)', *Australian Dictionary of Biography*, National Centre of Biography, Australian National University, adb.anu.edu.au/biography/moncrieff-gladys-lillian-7621/text13319.

Bolton, G.C., 'Courtney, Victor Desmond (1894–1970)', *Australian Dictionary of Biography*, National Centre of Biography, Australian National University, adb.anu.edu.au/biography/courtney-victor-desmond-9841/text17407.

Find a Grave, database and images, findagrave.com/memorial/90545088/audrey-campbell-sinclair, memorial page for Audrey Campbell Jacob Sinclair (9 February 1905 – 5 November 1970), Find a Grave Memorial ID 90545088, citing Santa Barbara Cemetery, Santa Barbara, Santa Barbara County, California, USA; Maintained by Ron West (contributor 47389384).

Fremantle Prison, 'The Convict Era', fremantleprison.com.au/history-heritage/history/the-convict-era.

Heritage Council, InHerit, 'Government House and Grounds', heritage report, 2021, inherit.stateheritage.wa.gov.au/Public/Inventory/Details/41687ad7-fb08-45d0-9e16-cb71480eb3f2.

King, Hazel, 'Armfield, Lillian May (1884–1971)', *Australian Dictionary of Biography*, Australian National University, adb.anu.edu.au/biography/armfield-lillian-may-5050.

National Archives and Records Administration (NARA); Washington, DC; *Marriage Reports in State Department Decimal Files, 1910–1949*; Record Group: *59, General Records of the Department of State, 1763–2002*; Series ARC ID: *2555709*; Series MLR Number: *A1, Entry 3001*; Series Box Number: *527*; File Number: *133*, accessed online at Ancestry.com. *US, Consular Reports of Marriages, 1910–1949* [database online]. Provo, UT, USA: Ancestry.com Operations, Inc.

Parliament of Western Australia, 'Members' biographical register: Alfred Bowman Kidson', parliament.wa.gov.au/parliament/library/MPHistoricalData.nsf/(Lookup)/47D5CF2A511239CA482577E50028A697?).

Parliament of Western Australia, 'Hubert Stanley Wyborn Parker', parliament.wa.gov.au/parliament/library/MPHistoricalData.nsf/(Lookup)/17E7B8F9C01843A1482577E50028A75A?OpenDocument.

Texas Department of Health, Audrey Sinclair's death certificate, State File No. 90382, available through ancestry.com, ancestry.com.au/discoveryui-content/view/615802:2272.

Western Australian Parliament, *Police Act (1892–1967)*, sections 65, 66 and 67, legislation.wa.gov.au/legislation/prod/filestore.nsf/FileURL/mrdoc_17653.pdf/$FILE/POLICE%20ACT%201892%20-%20%5B03-00-00%5D.pdf?OpenElement.

ALSO AVAILABLE

Josie de Bray was a brothel madam who owned most of Roe Street, Perth from World War I up to the 1940s. This immensely readable social history focuses the life of Josie de Bray as a conduit into the lives of her friends and competitors—the many women who paraded in their petticoats on the verandas of Roe Street, who were kept from the public view, and who were secret keepers themselves on the seamy side of town.

FROM FREMANTLEPRESS.COM.AU

FROM FREMANTLE PRESS

In 1907, Alice Mitchell was arrested for the murder of five-month-old Ethel Booth. During the inquest and subsequent trial, the public was horrified to learn that at least 37 infants had died in Mitchell's care in the previous six years. It became clear she had been running a 'baby farm', making a profit out of caring for the children of single mothers and other 'unfortunate women'. This book retraces this infamous 'baby farm' tragedy and a trial which gripped the nation and led to legislative changes to protect children's welfare.

AND ALL GOOD BOOKSTORES

ALSO AVAILABLE

San Francisco, 1856. Irish-born James 'Yankee' Sullivan is being held in jail by the Committee of Vigilance, which aims to rout the Australian criminals from the town. As Sullivan's mistress seeks his release and his fellow prisoners are taken away to be hanged, the convict tells a story of triumph and tragedy: of his daring escape from penal servitude in Australia; how he became America's most celebrated boxer; and how he met the true love of his life.

FROM FREMANTLEPRESS.COM.AU

FROM FREMANTLE PRESS

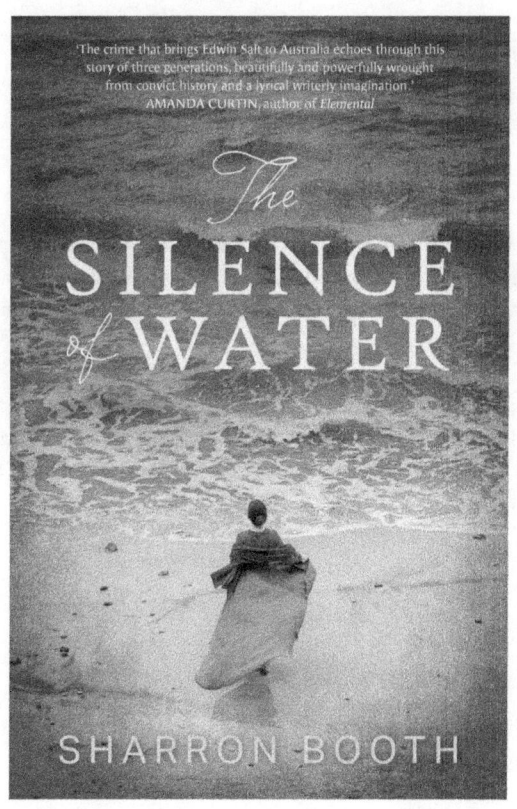

When Agnes announces her family is moving to Western Australia to take care of her father, Agnes' daughter finds herself a stranger in a new town living in a home whose currents and tensions she cannot understand. But Fan forms a suprising alliance with her grandfather. As she listens to memories of his life in England before he was transported as a convict, Fan begins to snoop through his belongings in an attempt to fill the gaps in his stories. The secrets she uncovers will change her family forever.

AND ALL GOOD BOOKSTORES

First published 2022 by
FREMANTLE PRESS

Fremantle Press Inc. trading as Fremantle Press
PO Box 158, North Fremantle, Western Australia, 6159
www.fremantlepress.com.au

Copyright © Leigh Straw, 2022

The moral rights of the author have been asserted.

This book is copyright. Apart from any fair dealing for the purpose of private study, research, criticism or review, as permitted under the *Copyright Act*, no part may be reproduced by any process without written permission. Enquiries should be made to the publisher.

Cover images: Dance At Government House Ballroom, State Library of Western Australia, b2405110_1; Studio portrait of Miss Jacob 30 July 1921, SLWA, slwa_b2572229_3; Cyril Gidley, trove.nla.gov.au/newspaper/article/76443278
Designed by: Carolyn Brown, tendeersigh.com

 A catalogue record for this book is available from the National Library of Australia

ISBN 9781760990572 (paperback)
ISBN 9781760990589 (ebook)

Fremantle Press is supported by the Western Australian State Government through the Department of Cultural Industries, Tourism and Sport.

Fremantle Press respectfully acknowledges the Whadjuk people of the Noongar nation as the traditional owners and custodians of the land where we work in Walyalup.